FOLLOW ME

Barbara!

Thank you so
much for joining the
life of pilgrims!

Peace
Brett Webb-Mitchell

FOLLOW ME

CHRISTIAN GROWTH
ON THE PILGRIM'S WAY

BRETT WEBB-MITCHELL

CHURCH PUBLISHING
an imprint of
Church Publishing Incorporated, New York

Library of Congress Cataloging-in-Publication Data

Webb-Mitchell, Brett.
    Follow me : Christian growth on the pilgrim's way / Brett
Webb Mitchell.
        p. cm.
    ISBN-13: 978-1-59627-025-1
    ISBN-10: 1-59627-025-X
    1. Christian life. 2. Spiritual life – Christianity. 3. Christian
pilgrims and pilgrimages. 4. Webb-Mitchell, Brett. 5. Christian
biography.
    I. Title.
    BV4501.3.W388 2006
    263′.041 – dc22

                                                            2006024432

Church Publishing Incorporated
445 Fifth Avenue
New York, NY 10016
www.churchpublishing.org

5 4 3 2 1

To Dean

Contents

ACKNOWLEDGMENTS

During the many pilgrimages I've taken around the world, I've carried a small book of pilgrimage practices and rituals. This book was given to me on the first pilgrimage I took to Chimayo, New Mexico, and has remained a constant in all the pilgrimages I've taken ever since. In the opening ritual of the pilgrimage, "The Blessing of Pilgrims upon Their Departure," there is a simple prayer with a refrain that has stood out for me as a radical call: "Lord, be the companion of our journey." Imagine us, God's people, calling on Jesus to be on our journey! Shouldn't it be the other way around, waiting to be called on the journey *with Jesus?* Of course, Jesus *has* already called us to be on the journey toward heaven's gates, and it is our awakening from our earthly slumber to realize that we are on an exciting adventure with none other than Jesus himself by our side. Jesus is our constant companion.

The way I discovered this truth is through the good company and rollicking fellowship I experience during the pilgrimages I have been on since 1999. Father Ed and Deacon Don were great pilgrim guides on the way to El Santuario de Chimayo; the brothers of the Abbey of the Crucified Christ, home to El Cristo Negro, the Black Christ, like Brother Robert along with the Capriel family, welcomed me with open arms of friendship. Mary in Pettigo, Ireland, treated me with a kindness that made this stranger feel like a welcome guest. And the Judith and David Banks family of

Nottinghamshire, England, have always received me as an extended part of their growing family.

My thanks also go to the Association of Theological Schools, Pittsburgh, Pennsylvania. In 2000 I received a grant for studying pilgrimage as a way of educating Christians when I was a full-time seminary faculty member. This gift gave me an opportunity to broaden my vision of pilgrimage-as-education. This book is but one of many fruits of this grant, which also enabled me to take many of the students from my seminary classes on pilgrimage at the end of each semester. Thank you all for coming along on the journey.

Thanks to Richard Rodriguez, who helped me understand the beauty of writing personal essays on pilgrimage; to Sister Stefanie Weisgram for reading, editing, and encouraging me to go on more pilgrimages; to Wally Hannum, who, on my return home would always ask me, "Where are you going next?"; to my parents, Liz and Don, who gave me the joy of traveling; to Jerry Eidenier, who taught me the poetry of words; to Rita Bennett and Matt Norvell, students-now-friends, who have joined me in many pilgrimages and believe in the Pilgrim God; to Frank Tedeschi, who saw something meaningful in this collection of essays; and to Paul Ilecki, who was responsible for getting me to go on the first pilgrimage to Chimayo.

Finally, many thanks to Dean and to my children, Parker and Adrianne, who kept the house together on my frequent journeys. For your prayers and well-wishes, I am eternally thankful.

INTRODUCTION

Go from your country and your kindred and your father's house to the land that I will show you. —Genesis 12:1

As will become plainly obvious in reading this book, my pilgrimage began when I least expected it. I did not go out and look for ways to become a pilgrim. It more or less feels like my becoming a pilgrim is a happy accident, or so it feels to me, now that I understand and appreciate that I am a pilgrim of God. Being a pilgrim and going on pilgrimage is an unintentional but gladsome development in my life. After all, I am simply following in the footsteps of none other than Sarah and Abraham, who were called by God to go on pilgrimage, "to a land that I will show you" (Gen. 12:1), and I am following the paradigmatic Pilgrim God, Jesus Christ (Brother Roger of Taizé).

The idea of partaking in the practice, and later the art, of pilgrimage, especially Christian pilgrimage, was not something that I went to, but the idea came *to* me, blocking my every twist and turn away from such a practice. Since going on my first pilgrimage to El Santuario de Chimayo, the images, symbols, rituals, prayers, and songs of pilgrimage now accompany me each and every day. And because I came to see myself as a pilgrim of God, I now know that it is in the serendipitous nature of the Holy Spirit that I see most clearly the ways of pilgrimage in daily life.

For example, when I accompanied a group of Presbyterian college students to the Dominican Republic I was surprised by the image of the Black Christ, El Cristo Negro, that I first encountered on a pilgrimage to Esquipulas, Guatemala, home of the original Black Christ in Central America and the Caribbean. The stories of St. Cuthbert and St. Aidan, written by the Venerable Bede, gained enormous importance by my being on the Holy Isle of Lindisfarne during an early spring research trip on pilgrimage. Their stories became alive in ways not easily put into words while I was walking the shoreline of Lindisfarne, or sitting overlooking the cemetery on that windswept isle, imagining the presence of those early pioneers of Christian pilgrimage. Finally, I could have sworn I saw the footsteps of St. Patrick himself on the isle in the middle of Lough Derg in Northern Ireland as I walked in the cold night air along the rocky shore for at least nine times in twenty-four hours.

More important, the lessons of pilgrimage continue to be played out in my daily life. For example, there are the lessons of patience that I first encountered in long walks on pilgrimage, waiting for food, for a rest break in a day that would seem to stretch on for hours. In the daily rush of my life, when I demanded from God an immediate answer to my queries — my "why God?" times in situations that had no easy answers — I soon realized that I would have to be patient in awaiting a resolution to such inquiries. I had to remind myself that *life* is a pilgrimage in which I would have to be patient with some long hours and days in which there were no quick answers to my more complex problems. Other virtues that were nurtured and further shaped on actual pilgrimages would also come to the fore: perseverance when I wanted to get something accomplished quickly; self-control when I would rather have lashed out in rage over someone's actions; and anticipation of the unexpected in-breaking of God's presence in moments when I least expected it. The radicalness was all of the Holy Spirit's doing, not of my own. Hospitality was extended to me whenever I needed it, or even when I did not know I needed it. But I was grateful for its practice whenever I sat down long enough to catch my breath.

This book is a collection of essays that detail my awakening to an often hidden truth: that the Christian life is a lifelong pilgrimage. It is a pilgrimage that began before we were born, a movement of God's people throughout time, of which we are but the most recent pilgrims. It is a pilgrimage that we were not only born into, but our entrance was made public by our baptism, a gesture that reaches back to the practices of John the Baptist himself. It is a pilgrimage in which we are guided and accompanied by none other than Jesus Christ, the prototypical Pilgrim. But Christ is known primarily through the other members of the body of Christ, with whom we are co-sojourners. Life is a pilgrimage that is communal rather than solitary, though there are times and stretches of land and relationships in which it may feel like we are alone in the desert. But even as a Protestant, I have to come to understand that we are surely accompanied by Christ's Spirit and the communion of saints, for we are part of the visible and invisible church. As I came to depend on prayer at certain hours of the day, I have tried to replicate such a practice in my daily life as well at home or when traveling to various conferences. The rituals — be they sacramental or daily — that were heightened on the pilgrim's way continue to grow in importance in my daily walk in the faith of our forebears. The land, the very topography of this walk of faith, continues to grab hold of my imagination, drawing me to lean closer and listen more intently to the changes of the seasons. I read Scripture differently now, in that I and my life story are held up by the light of Scripture, and I can see in what ways my life, and the life of my family and friends, is or is not aligned with Scripture. Being on an actual pilgrimage, time and again, teaches me that the lessons of faith are not for the "head" or for academic and intellectual stimulation. Instead, pilgrimage involves our head, mind, body, spirit, heart, soul, the heel of the foot, and the blisters on toes — in other words, the pilgrimage of life is not a lesson for the mind, but for our entire being. Finally, our pilgrimage of life is one of continual lessons as we learn daily how to enact and perform aright the gestures of God's grace with the people we meet, and in the circumstances in which we find ourselves. Some times our gestures fall right in line with Scripture's stories, while at other times we discover our own shortcoming through either the performance, or lack thereof, in meeting the deep needs of the world on any given day. My willingness to obey God has improved markedly as I come to see and understand that this pilgrimage is where the lessons of life and love, faith and hope in the face of despair, joy amid struggle, are all to be encountered.

This book is itself organized roughly by the various movements of a pilgrimage. In an article by the Benedictine monk David Leftwich, he suggested the following movements of pilgrimage: the first chapter, "An Inkling," explores in depth the very first impulse to be on pilgrimage. The next move is the decision to be on pilgrimage, followed soon by the first step of a pilgrimage. For me, this took place in deciding to go be a pilgrim to El Santuario de Chimayo. This is followed by the journey itself, and the ups and downs, the periods of elation and times of great drought in sensing none of the first élan of being on pilgrimage. The final chapter,

"On the Road to Damascus...Virginia," is a destination chapter, one of the final moves of pilgrimage: getting to the place where we intended to go to on our pilgrimage.

Yet the pilgrimage and the sense of being a pilgrim do not end when the pilgrimage is over. What I have come to understand now is that an intentional or actual pilgrimage is but a time-intense pedagogical maneuver, of God's own creative way of teaching us, intended to teach us, one and all, that we are on a pilgrimage of life, with the lessons of life arising from the very ground over which we move, thus imprinting us with the sign of the cross of Christ and expanding our awareness of God's Spirit in all of life.

Join me in these first musings on the possibility of being called to a pilgrimage of life....

Chapter One

An Inkling

If a man wants to be sure of his road, he must close his eyes and walk in the dark. — St. John of the Cross

Morning Impressions of Earthly Pilgrimage

It is an early, warm, autumn morning. I alone am awake in the stillness of the slowly dawning hours of the household. I hear my son snore softly upstairs from his bedroom, while across the hall my daughter turns over in bed, her bed sheets making a soft swishing noise. Not even our dogs notice such a gentle sound. As if I am sleepwalking, I mumble through morning prayers in the large, overstuffed armchair in the dark living room. No squares or rectangles of sunshine fall on the living room floor. All is a comfortable darkness. Stillness. Rest-filled quiet. My only companions are our dogs, who turn a sleepy eye my direction as I rustle the onion-paper pages in the prayer book and, in hushed tones so no one else awakes, while letting sleeping dogs lie, I pray softly the words to the Lord's Prayer. "Amen," I mutter to no one in particular. The collective response of the dogs is a snort. They blink their droopy eyes closed. Silence. Unstirring rest.

No one else is awake within the darkened Cape Cod–style house on this gentle hill. Rubbing early morning sleep from my tired eyes, I leave the sleeping house behind, opening and closing the front door with only a slight click from the lock itself as I turn it and shut the door. Soon I am trotting, almost stumbling, behind Lil, my overly enthusiastic young Labrador who leads the way to the empty street at the bottom of the sloping gravel driveway. The new chocolate Lab pup, Toby James, halts the bumbling procession to relieve himself on the weed-filled lawn, and soon catches up with Lil. From afar I see the slender shiny white plastic sleeve that holds the newspaper tightly. It lies at the bottom of the driveway, almost in the road. The newspaper unfurls quickly as I take it out of its protective girdle-like sleeve. The headline blares: "War Breaks Out in the Middle East," as it has for decades now.

I glance up and look eastward along the now-quiet country road, a place far removed from war's hellish wrath. This road gently passes by the front of my house. The asphalt roadway swoops up and glides to the left, toward the east, tall trees straddling either side, disappearing quickly at the horizon's edge. The forest of trees with their gnarly limbs and massive trunks provides an interesting textured canvas for the morning's first light. The light is slowly piercing the veil of a dusky morning mist. The trees and thick green and yellow bosk are beginning to be splashed with a Monet-like watercolor wash, with pastel shades of pink, red, and yellow of sunlight's serendipitous splashy debut showing off the start of the day. It is a movie trailer for the day to come. The late George Harrison's simple, melodic Beatle tune and words, "Here comes the sun, little darling," floats through my memory. I smile and start to hum it. "It's all right," I sing.

Lil is looking down the road with me as Toby James sniffs the new morning dew for any signs of nocturnal visitors. While Toby's attention is elsewhere, Lil and I face the

18

east. It is as if we are expecting someone, something, to arrive down the road. She senses something coming, her sleek body stiffened and poised, her black nose twitching, catching scents along the invisible rushing river of smells that only she can discern. Her smart brown eyes are fastened onto the dawning horizon. Her sitting posture is regal, as if she is looking over her vast kingdom, is well pleased, and is expecting guests at any time. Toby sniffs incessantly around our feet. He springs onto her back, like Charles Schultz's beagle Snoopy imitating a vulture, and Lil's concentration is gone. Around my legs the playful dogs vie for my attention and affection, their leashes entwining me, as if I were a squat maypole. With both of them playing underfoot, now out of the leash snare, I trundle back up to the house, newspaper in my arms.

The Earth's Pilgrimage

The earth is on a pilgrimage. I sense it in the sudden hint of warm Indian summer breeze picking up, disturbing the cooler autumn morning calm that preceded it. It is an almost sultry breeze upon my unshaven face, a remnant of summer's hot, hazy, and humid dog days. Some of the pages of the open newspaper under my right arm rustle freely. The soon-to-be-falling leaves flap together fast enough to make a whishing, stirring, almost white static noise. There is almost a rhythm to the movement of nature. Sometimes, when the wind is strong enough, the limbs high in the trees will reach over and clack-clack against each other high over my head, sounding like large South American claves hitting one another to the rhythm of the wind. The rustling and clacking sound make such a racket that it seems like a vehicle is coming down the road toward us, when all it is is a steady breeze.

In Leonard Bernstein and Stephen Sondheim's Broadway musical *West Side Story*, one of the gang members sings about something stirring, "Who knows? Could be . . . might be?" Something is happening, coming my way. Something might happen today.

The blacktop of the roadway, with its yellow stripe in the middle, resembles a large skunk. My sandaled feet are moist, laden with dew as I follow my dogs on their walk in the high, brown grasses in the front of the house. For a moment I stand there, the road vacant of cars, taking in the growing intensity of the bright morning on this fine new day. A scenic morning vista is being created before my very eyes. Layer upon layer of watercolor pastels are piling on top of each other now, one color washing, blurring into the next. Now it looks like a William Turner watercolor, in which there is only a vague sense of what is coming into focus. Yet even if I stand still enough, I won't catch the Painter, the Musician, and the Creator at work. The Artist works stealthily, serenely, seemingly enjoying the game of cat and mouse with us creatures, planted upon this creation. The Artist is a blithe spirit.

Back to earth: I cannot take my eye, my mind, my imagination off the smooth gliding curve ahead, and the echo of shuffling leaves and tree limbs moving against each other. Nature is telling me something; someone is coming this way. The curve ahead is all mystery. The curve is a portal, a tunnel, in which all I can see are the coming headlights of the sun. As headlights reach ahead of the car, searching its future path, so the sun's bright rays reach me even before I can see the beaming, roaring sphere of hot gases and fire rising above the tree line. The sun is always coming around that certain bend in the road, yet always surprising me by never hitting the road itself, but glancing off of it like a flat pebble skimming the surface of a still lake. The sphere of fire and light and movement rises above me, hovering above and off the road, above the underbrush, over the trees, sloping over and around the hills, the mountains, of North Carolina. Soon the clouds are below the sun's mighty far-reaching splish-splash of yellow-orange daylight. It is all drama, this unpretentious presentation of the molten, churning, fire-spewing morning sun. It is no wonder that other civilizations have invented or invited sun gods to herald the beginning of the day, a beardless, young, white-robed Apollo to take the sun over the arc of sky, four muscular horses pulling the fiery chariot ablaze in splendorous light. In the Psalms, God is compared to the sun, and at the moment of his transfiguration Jesus' face shone like the sun.

The hymn "Immortal invisible God only wise, in light inaccessible hid from our eyes," jumps to mind, switching unconsciously to the verse "when we've been there ten thousand years, bright shining as the sun" of "Amazing Grace." Tunes and melodies I've learned in the past are sparked into consciousness, depending on circumstances. As a musician I am like a small juke box on the diner's table, with events as the quarter to get me to sing a tune.

As the sun gives the impression of rising as the earth gradually rotates along its seemingly predestined pathway — a pathway well-understood and mapped by Galileo — the curve of the road up ahead seems to beckon to me. It is short of being a clarion call. An adventure is before me. The road and the sun hold me in their strangely hypnotic gripping power. I am in a trance, caught up in wondering what is coming around that bend in the road. It is more than a car. Is there something or someone I don't know about coming around the bend? Perhaps I am the unexpected presence on the bend upon an otherwise straight and narrow road? I have an inkling that my future is out there, in the woods, around the bend, on the road.

The brightness of a new day's dawning, light dispelling darkness, creates and washes out shadows, clearing away the dark of night. The earth gently rolls over, end over end, without end, its poles keeping us steady as we go, ballast for the trip around the sun. The light of the morning sun saturates the darker, muted colors of the coming quiet rest of earth's slow autumnal growth in this hemisphere. Hibernation is soon to be on the menu for nature in this part of the world. Change is afoot. All is movement from and toward. Turning and churning. All is motion, out of our control. A cycle is commencing and yet continuing on. Even when standing still we move, are being moved, with or without a conscious awareness or a simple acknowledgement. We cannot stop this ceaseless rolling motion. To stay with the sun's bright ray on planet earth we would need to travel quite quickly, over land and sea.

Once, when flying from Sydney to Los Angeles in the daytime, I watched us fly toward the light of day with almost the absence of night. We were flying into a new day. But in staying right where we are on the Planet Earth Ride, are we not like children belted into a slow rolling Ferris wheel riding unconsciously on the planet's constant roll? Or are we on a slightly tilting, twirling planet, following a course that varies with each orbit and rotation, making our journey more like a roller coaster ride?

With fascination I watch shadows grow, widen, and fade away into light or complete darkness. In his book *In Praise of Shadows* Jun'ichiro Tanizaki calls me to observe with awe the shadows that move so gracefully in coordination of human and inanimate action. Tanizaki writes that shadows have that "glow of grime," providing for a "sheen of antiquity." Shadows are the only clear proof we have that we are moving, whether we like it, control it, or not. The earth's pilgrimage is peppered with shadows and sunlight, moonbeams and storms.

A Child's Love of the Journey

My focus on pilgrimage and journey was nurtured in me as a child. I incessantly questioned my parents as to how Mary Martin as Peter Pan could lose a shadow. On our black and white Zenith television set, one could see clearly the flirtatious and flitting shadow. In the evening, watching that musical, I looked over at my shadow. My shadow never left me. Where did Peter get such a flighty shadow? Is the shadow my soul? Peter Pan awoke the sleeping Darling children in their comfortable London beds in his hot pursuit of his independent-minded shadow. Can my shadow run away? Can I run away from my shadow? With needle and thread Wendy slowly sewed it back on for him. With the slightest movement possible, shadows move, change shape, lengthen, widen, to a point that all there is is the darkness of the shadow. All becomes shadow, and there is no light. The shadow disappears with the aid of the sun's withdrawal as darkness hastens on, only to return in another twelve hours or so. How fast is the speed of light? It is faster than the speed of sound. But how fast is that?

I have discovered another way to gauge the speed of our revolving planet. Friends tell me that on a cloudless, star-strewn night, if you lie down on a blanket in an open meadow and remain as still as possible, looking straight up into the canopy of sky, galaxy, universe, overhead, you get the slightest sensation of actually moving ever so slowly. I am out in the backyard, stretched out on my back, toes pointing up in the air, arms spread out. One friend admitted that she found herself rolling over on her stomach, pressing down harder and harder on the earth's grassy haircut, clutching rocks and digging in her toes, flesh touching soil of mother earth, trying desperately to cling to the rolling ball and not fall up. Watching shadows move, grow larger, more ominous, we see in what ways our life on this planet is ever moving, marching onward, or slouching along, whether we choose to move with the syncopation of it or not.

As inhabitants of this planet, this rolling, changing, evolving spheroid in the spinning galaxy known as the Milky Way, Buckminster Fuller called us space travelers moving through the cosmos on the spaceship earth. But by *naming* the earth as a spaceship in a way makes this world no longer the creation of the Creator's own fertile and radical imagination. Claiming it as our spaceship brings it to human dimensions, our creation, fashioned from our human ingenuity, know-how, and sometimes destructive tendencies. "If you put your mind to it, you can solve anything" was the motto for my generation, and our hope as we face seemingly irreversible changes upon this planet we call home. We are a generation fed on the hope born of the Enlightenment and the power of the individual and one's mind. But the Saturn rockets of the Apollo and space shuttle missions and the Sputnik satellites of my youth don't look like earth. They pale in comparison. Look at the spindly legs of Sputnik, or the spidery apparatus of the moon landing module. How odd they all are in comparison to this planet's large spherical shape, which looks like a large blue-green-white marble from the moon's crusty, dusty, rocky surface.

I was told once that Europeans understood pilgrimage as travel among a people, often conquering them along the way, like the Crusades. Early settlers in what we now call America perceived pilgrimage as a journey over land, going from east to west. We are only just now acknowledging our connection to those who are north and south of us. In the last century, our American pilgrimage has taken us up into space, to go places where "no one has gone before," says the captain of the starship *Enterprise*. I am a child of the television series *Star Trek* and the *Star Wars* movies, and I understand and dream that the pilgrimage is now to places where no one has gone before. I am the son of John Glenn and brother to Sally Ride. Perhaps Christians — Protestant or Catholic, it matters not — should consider that we are pilgrims over land, among people, through space, and over the tick-tock of time.

Hints of journey, of pilgrimage, are scattered throughout my earlier life in the Christian tradition. Consider the hymns in our hymnals: the church's song book is loaded with songs for the journey ahead. In elementary grades in Sunday school we learn the simple lyrics "Swing low, sweet chariot, coming for to carry me home." My father would sing in the shower or driving the old Buick "We are climbing Jacob's ladder" or "Onward, Christian Soldiers," in full operatic voice. I knew he was contented when he sang that song. When I attend worship at a small "radical" United Methodist church in Chicago, for our Benediction we sang — in Spanish — and marched to "We are marching to the light of Christ, we are marching to the light of Christ." The traffic of palm branches on Palm Sunday always makes a happy day for children given permission to let loose and let it all "hang out" in the sometimes uptight

Protestant and Catholic worship. Adults are envious at such celebrations.

Whether in our most alert, waking moments, in comfort under night's blanket, playing with children on our knees, caught up in the solitude of prayer, or clutching one another in an amorous embrace — regardless of our actions, our moves, our desires, we are involuntarily part of earth's ceaseless journey around the magnetic embrace of the sun. It is as if the earth were like a child attached to the parent's apron strings; we careen around in an orbit, ensnared by the sun's hypnotic pull. It makes us all travelers in space, pilgrims of the universe, riding upon a blue and green and brown and white and red and black marble.

Growing Up a Pilgrim; Seeing Life as Pilgrimage

I have come to see, to hear, to bear witness, to tell and write of my dawning awareness, born and bred of experience, that our life is a journey upon this God-created, soil-encrusted, heavily-watered, grassy-meadowed, desert-spotted, tree-festooned, people-crowded swampy sphere. Whether we are willing riders or not, we are travelers — a traveling circus sideshow — or utterly strange bedfellows who are thrown together by the sheer coincidence that we are co-pilgrims on a journey through time and space and people and events both in and beyond our control. On more pleasant days, I consider us to be more or less like Geoffrey Chaucer's merry and not-so-merry band of pilgrims, who were thrown together because of their seeming devotion to going to the shrine of Thomas à Becket in Canterbury's cathedral. While seeing my life as a mish-mash of the monk's tale and the tale of the wife of Bath, I am caught up in living life amid many who are still in search of a story to give them some alternatives to live their life by.

On lonely days, this journey seems like a solitary one. An acquaintance told me the story of walking the long stretch of road to Santiago de Compostela in Spain. The hardest days for her were in the middle of a wheat field that seemed to go on forever. There was no break between azure sky and straw-yellow field. An ocean of blue sky overhead. No one around for miles. Two days walking. Three days walking. No one. She had sung every song, prayed every prayer, and recited all the Bible verses, poems, short stories, and advertisement jingles she knew. The immensity of land and sky was overwhelming her, engulfing her. She was like John Bunyan's pilgrim, "Christian," with no Evangelist to save her. She was fearful that she would drown and be swallowed up by the ocean of sky overhead.

Whether we are surrounded by others or strike out on our own, human life is about journeys and travels. There is always a certain sense, an inkling within that propels us to travel, to journey, to move on, to be part of a caravan, a throng; a vagabond existence waits for us. The tourists with Shirley Temple on the "Good Ship Lollipop." We are always either going to something, someplace, somewhere, or leaving it all behind. To go forward means to leave something, someone behind. To go deeper means to get under the surface of the thin, brittle veneer of life in order to see the immense and yet beautiful streams of life's complexities. To stay in one place is impossible. Remaining still or the same is not an option.

Old trick: stand by a creek: the water rushing past you, with all matter of debris and fish and tadpole, is not the same water. It doesn't recycle itself in exactly the same pattern.

Besides, we've just aged a minute, an hour, a day, a week, a month, a year.

Such traffic of life is the material of life itself. Sometimes we are passing through a land, a people, a certain time or situation, for all manner of reasons, voluntarily and often involuntarily. Yet the land, the people, the situations pass through us as well, leaving their sometimes smudgy thumbprint or an elegant mark upon our lives, one traveler to another.

I am aware of the truth of this observation every few years, when we are treated to the spectacular Leonid meteor shower. The shower of seemingly moving, shooting stars is thrilling as we watch from our cushy earthbound seats, with mouths agape yet smiling, emitting an "ooh" and "ahh" as this belt of meteors gives us a free, all-expenses paid, living drama and showy fireworks every few years. We are passing through this belt of soaring meteors as they are passing through us. Mark Twain marked his birth and death by the coming and going of a Haley's Comet. Whether we like to admit it or not, we are born to travel. We are born to be travelers. In the 1960s, we were told we were "born to be wild." Traveling has such an effect upon people.

To consider all of life a journey of some kind is perhaps an inelegant way of comprehending, of naming the constant motion of life. Whether I am the one moving, I am part of a group of people moving, or I am being moved by virtue of where I live, there is a constant motion forward through time and space, place and people. To explain, to understand, to wrap our small minds and limited intellects around the constant movement of our life and life around us, we have used the rhetoric of journey, travel, trek, tour, outing, wandering, or more mysterious words full of potential surprises:

quest, flight, voyage, odyssey, junket, traverse, globe trot, rove, pilgrimage.

We clock each day with the language of a trip. The journey begins with a quick: "I'm off, honey!" as we race out of our homes through the door of the house to our cars or minivans, the subway, our bicycles or scooters, or the school bus. We are leaving the known to be clasped into the arms of the unknown. We make a trek to a certain place with certain people, where we spend hours throughout the day. For many, it has become customary to see morning as a period of leaving, taking off to join the traveling horde of others like us: children and adults, women and men, blue- and white-collared workers whom we will see that day. When calling someone at home or work or school, we need to ask, "Do you have a minute?" as often the other person is moving onward to the next task, the next meeting, the next class. Cellular phones make it all that much easier to catch a person on the move. It's a shame: there is nothing to tell at the end of the day if we've been telling each other our stories all the while. No time for reflection, or a chance to nuance the heck out of a boring day. At close of day is the end of the journey when we say, "Honey, I'm home!" We end where we begin, but we are not the same. Nor are the people we live with. In casual conversations, at the end of the day, week, or month, we mention and recount to others in our homes what a long road we feel we have walked down, putting our feet up, ready to be massaged, for the vagabond life has left its mark upon our tattered soul.

We also use the rhetoric of journey, of pilgrimage, in order to understand the meandering passage of human life. For the sake of conformity, we establish theories of human development by which we understand that there is always a past that precedes what is present, pointing us toward a certain — or uncertain — future. We create time and clocks and calendars to help us navigate the uncharted journey of life. We age along a chronological pathway, with pre-established mile-markers set to days, months, years, and events in life. They can serve as helpful, user-friendly signs along the way to tell us where we are.

For example, according to the middle-class American script, we begin life with a debate: does life begin at birth or at conception? "On your mark, get set..." The period marked "infancy" is an age of romancing the child; "childhood" means we're not quite thirteen years old, still hold on to an innocence, and can get away with quite a lot, if we're cute and darling. "Teenage years": we're granted time to rebel as parents and society grit their teeth, and then we move on to "adulthood" and the lack of rebellion and the expectation of conformity. "Young adulthood": I married, we had children, and we bought a house. "Mid-life crises": been there, seen that, and loved it. I was soon divorced, bought a sporty red car. And where we are headed? "Old age," or AARP, *Modern Maturity,* and a nursing-home future along the continuum of care. Death we call the "end of life," with an abstract finish line. Some put their faith in the continuance of the odyssey in a place called heaven or the afterlife. We are stuck with a cartoon image of St. Peter sitting at a desk before an iron gate: a heavenly toll road, where you pay the attendant before you're allowed to move on down the road.

The simplicity of this middle-class life was captured well at the 1964–65 World's Fair in New York City. General Electric's exhibition was a Disney-created event that showed off the world of tomorrow by starting with the world of the past: the Carousel of Progress. It was a simple, clean, whole-some, white, middle-class American world. The audience sat in an auditorium that moved in a slowly revolving circle, passing various theater sets with animatronic vignettes being played out. Each scene was in the same house, with the same robotic characters, with the same names, having the same fights and the same fun. Even the animals never changed. No one aged. No one rose in economic class. No one ever retired or left school. No one was born, and no one died. No one was black. No one was brown. The only thing that changed was the cast of electrical appliances. The theme song? "It's a great, big beautiful tomorrow, coming on the path of every day." And Broadway's Annie sings, "Tomorrow!"

But the pleasant carousel breaks down in real life. Once the gears grind to a halt we get off the carousel and walk onto the traveling path of years. We might pick up on Robert Frost's poetic, metaphoric vision of life as one of two choices as the road splits and diverges into the woods. Life as "either-or," a crossroad, a fork in the road. There is always the choice of the well-worn trail, following many others who have trod down that certain path. With the Wizard of Oz as our guide, we ease on down broad avenues and yellow-bricked roads, a munchkin on either side of us, wishing us well as we get closer to the Emerald City. The trees and hedges, mown of their verdant luster, become controlled growth or topiary. The grassy path is beaten down to the hard brown earth that has been transformed into rock; the earth reveals the imprints of tire marks of cars and trucks. There is an exit ramp here and there, with blue signs of food, lodging, rest area, and gas at .2 miles to the right.

There is the other, less traveled path that few have trod. There is a high level of underbrush that we step over and vines hanging overhead. A spider or snake drops down for a visit. There is no clear pathway before us, or trail markers to assure us we are walking the correct direction. We frequently take out our rusty compasses and Shell gasoline road maps from our sweat-stained back pockets, searching for some direction, if we can figure out where are due north, south, east, or west, as we make a new path where few others, if any, have trod. Underbrush rules; trees are riddled with life; mystery prevails. We have serendipitous encounters with strangers who reveal the Holy as magnified in the life of those considered "least" among Christ's family. Breathtaking, jaw-bending vistas may be around the next bend without any notification or signs saying "Photo Op Next Turn." Now and then we find an item from civilization, garbage or debris, scattered fragments of one kind or another. Cameras swing around our necks. We rubberneck, hoping not to miss one unforgettable site. We clutch a map that we picked up at the trail's entrance and stuff it into our back pocket. Welcome to the pathway of the pilgrim.

What Is a Pilgrim? Where Is the Pilgrimage To?

Though there may be a roughly hewn, sketchy pathway for a pilgrimage, it is the encounters along the way that make us a pilgrim. Philip Cousineau reminds us of the root of the word "pilgrimage":

> *peligrinus* or foreigner or wayfarer, the journey of a person who travels to a shrine or holy place. Another older derivation, more poetic, reveals that pilgrim has its roots in the Latin *per agrum,* "through the field." This ancient image suggests a curious soul who walks beyond known boundaries, crosses fields, touching the earth, with a destination in mind and a purpose in heart. The pilgrim is a wayfarer who

longs to endure a difficult journey to reach the sacred center of his or her world, a place made holy by a saint, hero, or god.[1]

For the pilgrim, each day is the confrontation of the eternal paradox that is ever present before us: when we are still and silent we wish to be moving, and when we are moving forward we soon yearn to remain still and silent, discovering the quiet place where we no longer find ourselves bested by the ceaseless motion of the journey around the sun, let alone the brouhaha of daily existence. We find ourselves in the frantic search for T. S. Eliot's quiet, gentle still point of the turning world,

> Where past and future are gathered. Neither movement
> from nor towards,
> Neither ascent nor decline.[2]

Eliot describes the hope, but never let's us know if he got there.

A naval chaplain once boasted to me that in his church the military service personnel come to find their elusive still point. Yet finding the still point doesn't negate the truth that we are a people who are either on the move or being moved as we roll merrily along on earth's slowly spinning trail. Besides, the journey is not always outward, but more often inward, deeper and deeper into the uncharted nethermost world of our very souls, uncollected bits and pieces of an otherwise collective psyche, of archetypal matter, if you believe in such a place. Our neurotic fears and psychotic

---

1. Philip Cousineau, *Art of the Pilgrimage* (Berkeley: Conari Press, 1998), 13–14.
2. T. S. Eliot, *Four Quartets* (Orlando, FL: Harcourt, Brace & Co., 1971), 15.

wonders keep us on the edge of control. Yet the dragon of our innermost self takes us to places in our honeycomb collective lives where God alone can save us.

An Accidental Pilgrim

This reflection on sunshine, shadows, moving planets, journeying lives, restless bodies, travels that are either in our control or out of our control is sparked by actual life circumstances: I am an accidental pilgrim.

I am not a likely candidate for pilgrimage, though probably not least likely to call myself or be called a pilgrim. The rhetoric — let alone the practice — of pilgrim and pilgrimage was not in my repertoire or thesaurus of life experiences.

I was raised in a family who loved to travel. My childhood summers were spent in the back of a 1963 white Buick LeSabre, moving around the Northeast, visiting various historic sites of the Revolutionary and Civil Wars. As we ate our cold breakfasts in the early morning by the closed gates of numerous Presidential homes, my mother would jokingly tell us we were having breakfasts with presidents. At four in the afternoon each day, my brother and I were ready for a chocolate milkshake, a necessary luxury on those long car trips. The love of travel, of seeing new sites, meeting new people, sleeping in hotel rooms with color televisions (we had black and white), swimming in a pool, tasting different foods, was born, cradled, and nurtured deeply and lovingly by my parents.

But pilgrimage is different from such sightseeing or tourist expeditions. Huston Smith wrote that the purpose of pilgrimage is not "rest and recreation — to get away from it all. To set out on a pilgrimage is to throw down a challenge to everyday life. Nothing matters now but this adventure."[3] As an American Protestant — baptized in a Congregational church, raised as a United Methodist, becoming a middle-class Presbyterian in my adolescent years — I find the language and the practice of pilgrimage to be foreign. We Protestants don't do that kind of thing.

In the world in which I grew up, pilgrimage was something vaguely Catholic. We just didn't do that certain walk, let alone acknowledge the potency of relics and the myriad Santos adorning the walls and the phantasmagoric world of God spawned by excessive candles burning, seen only through grimy icons and sooty crosses and lifesize statues of Jesus in loincloth and blood, either on the way to the cross or on the cross or being lowered from the cross, dead.

Hiking, yes. Walking through museums and art galleries, yes. Presbyterians fly to visit John Calvin's place in Geneva, Switzerland, John Knox's St. Giles' pulpit in Edinburgh, Scotland. Meanwhile, I have run into Methodists sweating during their summer vacations while walking to Aldersgate St. near the Barbican Center in London in search of their Wesleyan experience of a strangely warmed heart. I am told that Lutherans like to go to Germany to seek out Martin Luther's steps toward revolution in the church, with hopes of buying a papery fragment of the theses nailed on a church door. Protestants and Catholics alike flock to the Holy Land to go on "pilgrimage" in air-conditioned buses and comfy stays at King David Hotel, with a certificate of authenticity on simulated parchment paper. But the rhetoric and act of pilgrimage is strange, if not a little too exotic, to my thoroughly Protestant understanding and upbringing of life.

---

3. Huston Smith in Cousineau, *The Art of Pilgrimage*, xi.

The first image of a pilgrim that I grew up with was the cast of one-dimensional characters who arrived on the *Mayflower* in 1620. We don't know them as individuals, but as the solitary group who floated over here on the brown wooden *Mayflower* and landed upon what is now called Plymouth Rock. Images of their tramping around on dark days, walking through the November snow in New England to encounter the aboriginal culture of this land are deeply imprinted upon our memories. In elementary school, I remember that boys wore black pants and shoes, with aluminum foil wrapped around cardboard squares for buckles, while the girls wore simple bonnets made of white construction paper. Others were chosen to be the Indians, with colorful feathers made of construction paper. We sing: "We gather together to ask the Lord's blessing. He hastens and chastens his will to make known." Those Pilgrims were very much the epitome of pilgrims on a pilgrimage to an unknown destination.

In high school I read Geoffrey Chaucer's stories of the pilgrims of Canterbury. I laughed and cried my way through the bawdy musical *Canterbury Tales* in the West End of London. Seminary church history courses briefly covered the salient historical points of the pilgrimage phenomenon in less than fifteen minutes. It was a Protestant seminary, so we had little invested in such "arcane practices." Pilgrimage was seen as a medieval mistake or frivolity as we discounted its merits, chortling at Martin Luther's invectives against pilgrimage as yet one more way to collect indulgences for building St. Peter's in Rome.

Rather than fully embracing and seeking information on pilgrimage, I was backed into a corner. My first pilgrimage was almost an accident, a lucky fluke, a predestined happenstance. In one of my books I have an essay on young people with disabilities being like pilgrims, lost, cast into an alien place, asking the community of Christians how to get out of the place they are stuck. Many of them were born and raised in homes in which one or both parents were abusive, while others were struggling with an addiction problem or mental illness that brought their young lives to a standstill, interrupting their growth into adulthood, let alone the wonders of adolescence. Without much reflective thought I borrowed a scenario not unlike that of the solitary pilgrim, Christian, in Bunyan's *Pilgrim's Progress,* to explain their lives. Like Bunyan's Christian, these young people spent an inordinate amount of time stuck in the Slough of Despond, which appeared to be a gross sandpit that resembled the muck and mire of these young people's lives.

My intellectual curiosity about pilgrimage grew in intensity over a relatively short period of time as I searched high and low for another, more inclusive way of understanding how we grow, change, learn, and know what we know. To borrow and paraphrase from the work of Parker Palmer, I was interested in how we know that we are known by God in Christ, especially if we don't have the same capacity to think, to feel, to intuit, to recognize, to hurt, to love, to be wounded, to be healed that is the stuff of life.

For example, does growing mean an accumulation of or sloughing off of ideas? Does one grow or expand into an awareness of life? Is growing going beneath the surface of the thin veneer of life, or rising above the ordinary and sublime? Do we grow by focusing on what matters, prioritizing, or living by the skin of our teeth?

I started to read pilgrimage narratives voraciously when I was looking for alternatives to complement theories of human development. Again, the generalized theme of pilgrimage seemed an interesting way to shape questions and to find answers — or responses — as I tried to understand human growth in all its complexities and thickness. I know, for certain, that growth is caused by more than a response to a single stimulus. Rather, growth occurs through an amazing network of stimuli and responses, known and unknown, with consciousness or Freudian unconsciousness, whether we know what the First Cause is or have hints about the innumerable secrets of what causes us to grow.

But the safety was in sitting back in the easy chair in the safe confines of a library reading room, in front of a computer screen, reading *about* pilgrimage from the safety of such an enclosure rather than being *on* a pilgrimage. While I do believe in the power of the written word to form and transform worlds through the metaphoric use of language, I was soon to find myself immersed in the practices of an actual pilgrimage.

The First Real, Live Pilgrimage!

It is early June 1999. I am in Costilla, New Mexico, on the border of southern Colorado. From a distance I can see the white-capped mountains. I was on my first "official" pilgrimage to the small adobe sanctuary in Chimayo, New Mexico — El Santuario de Chimayo. To say that this trip changed, and possibly saved, my life and that it has never been the same may sound grandiose and over the top. I am known for being dramatic, but it's also true. After this trek, pilgrimage was no longer an academic interest, a book or narrative from someone else's life. Pilgrimage became a living tradition that I was now integrally a member of as I learned to live into the identity of pilgrim. Gone was simple intellectual curiosity about the extraordinary formation of a person on pilgrimage. This was replaced by sore feet with blisters, aching knees, throbbing calves, tight shoulders, and aching back, yet also a vision of sights and colors, of orange and brown strata of rock formations and an ear for new sounds and eerie silences of desert places amid the New Mexican landscape that defied any glossy travel brochures for artist's escapes, skier's holidays, and white-water rafting trips.

Little did I know at the time I walked to Chimayo that this was the first of many pilgrimages that I would make in the coming years. Chimayo was followed by a pilgrimage of sorts to St. John's Abbey and University, and St. Benedict's Monastery in central Minnesota. There I found a writing life I had sadly left in pursuing other, less noble, prizes.

I found myself in unforgettable conversations with monks while observing the richly variegated life of pilgrims in the large white basilica in Esquipulas, Guatemala, as we all bowed before the beautiful carving known simply as El Cristo Negro — the Black Christ. Sitting on a fence rail, I poured out my heart to a silent chorus of age-worn tombstones on the Holy Isle of Lindisfarne. Only a few months later I was walking the pilgrim walk on the isle in Lough Derg, known as St. Patrick's Purgatory.

With each of these pilgrimages I found myself caught up in a certain set of rituals through which I would engage in pilgrimage: morning prayers, followed by a meal; midday prayer wherever I was; racing in for choral evening vespers if possible. I've the same green day pack for the many pilgrimages I've been on. I've always said a prayer, taken a deep breath, and taken that first step into a car, into a plane, onto a boat, onto an island, up a mountain, over to a church, with the same sense of immediacy and high level of expectations, laced with anxiety over the unknown that would greet me along the way. On pilgrimage I have always known that there was a destination, but I have never known exactly what all — or who all — I would meet along the way. Often I didn't even know what the destination looked like. I had only heard tales about them or read about a place in a book. All I could plan on was hope: hope of getting there, but I could never gauge what would be met along the way; hope of meeting interesting people, but I could never dictate who they would be; hope for a better understanding of a life of growth in pilgrimage, but I could never tell what was going to grow or why.

More surprising was the way that the themes of pilgrimage would become the filter, the template, the practice of my life in just a few years down the road from that first pilgrimage in New Mexico. Pilgrimage for me is how I understand my life in particular, and the Christian life overall. I would freak out more, drink more, take more medication — any medication — call up more friends, hesitate more, see a therapist more times than there are days in the week, be on bent knees more, if I didn't see, hear, move through, and schedule life for the pilgrimage that it is. Though I was raised in a home where self-discipline was a high virtue, I try valiantly and with little guilt or remorse to take life one step at a time without holding out the suspicion that I can make it move to my will. While I can work on gestures that may prepare me for circumstances ahead of me on the journey, I strive to see life as an unfolding event, in which the serendipitous reigns over the controlled and contrived. To that end I am learning when I can achieve some of my goals and learning to let go and be present when called to be in a certain place, letting the Spirit of God guide me in a certain, hopefully right, path. To that end, life is more than a tourist's road trip, or a Bob Hope–Bing Crosby–Ava Gardner tryst in Mandalay. Pilgrimage is the growth of a person resulting from an outward, exterior journey. It is more than a search for self, but a serious engagement of activities that deepen and strengthen one's grace-given relationship with the Holy. After all, this is what we most desire: to know, deep in our bones, that we are a new creation, open to the love of our eternal God.

"If a man wants to be sure of his road, he must close his eyes and walk in the dark," writes St. John of the Cross. With eyes closed I take the steps of a pilgrim. Though the day is often dark, the storied essays that follow are some lessons learned from the pilgrimages I've walked in the last two years. Each essay reveals an aspect of pilgrimage that seemed key in learning the awkward, often stilted, shuffling, traipsing, running, halting, walk of faith. Like St. John of the Cross, I learned to close my eyes and walk in the dark, in faith, rather than opening them up and grabbing control, thus proving to God that I did not trust him to guide me on the road before me.

It is night as I finish reworking this chapter yet one more time. The sun has settled in a land, a place, among a people not near here. For them it is morning. There is no summertime glow left upon this spot of earth. Autumn is here. Tonight there are new, different shadows outside my cabin window, crafted not by sunshine but the eerie blue-white glow of a full milky white moon. The moon's quietly stealthy movement across the backyard of my house speaks to me, like the sun, of travel, of time, of pilgrimage. I sing "Shine on Harvest Moon," to myself, an old gem of a song my family used to sing on long car trips in the Buick LeSabre of my youth. I go beyond an inkling about pilgrimage. I am a pilgrim; I am becoming a pilgrim, a wanderer, a wayfarer. A pilgrimage is afoot, to Chimayo!

Chapter Two

THE EDUCATION OF A PILGRIM
The First Step

Father, I abandon myself into your hands;
Do with me what you will;
Whatever you may do, I thank you;
I am ready for all, I accept all....
Into your hands I commend my soul.
— Brother Charles of Jesus

The education of a pilgrim begins with the simplest movement of the foot forward. There it is: in the very first step
going forward. There is nothing glamorous or stupendous
about this initial movement: no trumpet blasts heralding
the coming of yet one more pilgrim along a path. It all
took place in the hushed quiet of an early June morning.
The lowly, cracked heel rolls to the middle tender sole of
the foot. I am a suburban kid, and the soles of my feet are
tender as a baby's bottom. Striking the dusty ground with
one foot, and then the other, continually rolling heel to toe,
gently lifting up off the earth, I leave a fragmented and tem-
porary imprint upon the silt-like brown soil. The first gust
of a good wind, or pouring rain, and the print will vanish.
The education of a novice pilgrim's body continues as the
neural charges and synaptic nerve endings dance, and energy ascends and excites the vast web of arteries and veins
throughout my body. With the upturn of the ankle, the muscles of my calves contract slightly, causing knee to bend with

tendon's help and thigh to tighten, going forward and then back to a stride.

Invisible energy shoots up the torso, into the stubborn, curving, snake-like backbone. Pilgrimage soon encircles and shoots through my body and charges my mind with a panoply of images of pilgrimages of yore, until this amateur act of this wannabe pilgrim begins to sense a story being written into the marrow of backbone and the shaping of my tenderfoot soul. My heart can't wait to get further into the pilgrimage as it expands to welcome the waiting Spirit who silently accompanies me on this trek. God is the Creator of the very soil I traipse and the One who is watching overhead with eagle's eye. My eyes are drawn upward toward the cloudless blue heavens of New Mexico. A singular cottony wisp of cloud hangs lonely against the deep blue canvas of sky, lit by the rays of the full moon. I breathe in deeply, the sides of my nose indented; the smell of clear and fresh mountain air is intoxicating. The only sound I hear is the shushing of cloth rubbing against cloth: nylon against nylon sweats, or the denim of pant legs. The earth is moving beneath my foot: shuffled and crunched echoes in the nothingness of this deserted brown roadside trail.

With the host of other raggedy pilgrims I mutter with them a communal prayer I've never prayed before. It is three or four o'clock in the chill of the raven-black morning. I can't tell what time it is because the other day I was told to take off my watch by the spiritual director of the pilgrimage, Father Ed. The communal prayer continues: "And be with you also . . . I think," I mumble to no one in particular, surrounded by the daunting mountainous terrain of northern New Mexico. There is no coffee stand to awaken the dead. There isn't a car or truck driving by. There are no horses or mules on the nearby farms awake at this hour. No rooster is crowing the morning sun to awaken. No dog barks. No one is insane enough to be up at this godforsaken hour, except our shaggy band of pilgrims. The sign near the cafeteria door of the school we slept in overnight said "Costilla Elementary School." With no Toto the dog in sight I mutter, "We're not in Kansas anymore." What was I thinking of when I agreed to come on this lonely trek?

This odyssey began when I arrived in Taos via Albuquerque, New Mexico, on a Saturday afternoon. I flew in from bucolic, kudzu-infested, hot, hazy, and humid Chapel Hill, North Carolina. This June is hotter than usual, both in North Carolina and in New Mexico. But it is a different kind of heat in New Mexico. In the southeast, the summer air is as green as the variety of deciduous trees after a five o'clock thunderstorm. The air is sultry, thick with moisture, never allowing wet bathroom towels to dry out between showers. Life moves more slowly in such terrain. But in the southwest, the hot air is crisp to the touch. It is tinder dry. No moisture has a chance to withstand such an assault of dryness.

With the help of the airport van driver I found my way to the local Catholic church, where I met Father Ed. Father Ed's heritage as a Native American is a rich melange of many tribes, and yet he finds a home in the Catholic Church.

I still marvel at God's whimsy in leading me to this particular pilgrimage as the initial portal through which I would venture forth on many pilgrimages. It was here that I would start to see that my life specifically, and the life of Christians universally, is all a pilgrimage. The first suggestion that I go on pilgrimage came from conversations with my friend Paul, in North Carolina. Paul, a Paulist priest and a former Trappist monk, listened for many years to my seemingly endless babble and incessant curiosity *about* pilgrimage. I was an enthusiastic spectator of the theological and historical aspects of pilgrimage for many years before I came to New Mexico. Then one night, with little affect in his voice, Paul simply asked me the probing question, "You've never been *on* a pilgrimage, have you?"

I was quiet before this searching question. "No" I said with some embarrassment after a long pause.

That was the point: my knowledge of pilgrimage was babble, spoken by one who wasn't even a novice in such things. I was a master of ruminations, theological reflections, and endless intellectual speculation *about* pilgrimage from other people's perspectives: people who had never actually been on a pilgrimage, but nevertheless but written about pilgrimage from a historian's or theologian's point of view. My knowledge of pilgrimage was intellectual, an act of the mind, not bodily or spiritual. It was a division of mind dissociated from the bodily act or spiritual journey of pilgrimage.

As I write this I see on my good-size bookshelves a library full of pilgrimage narratives: tales by the Venerable Bede of St. Cuthbert's and St. Aidan's pilgrimages around Lindisfarne, England; Egeria's travel diary in the third century; John Bunyan's *Pilgrim's Progress;* Chaucer's *Canterbury Tales;* Sheri Holman's *The Stolen Tongue;* the poetry of T. S. Eliot; children's stories like George McDonald's *The Golden Key;* William Dalrymple's *From This Holy Mount;* Dorothy Day's *On Pilgrimage;* Paulo Coelho's *Pilgrimage;* Annie Dillard's *Pilgrim at Tinker Creek;* Belden Lane's *Solace of Fierce Landscapes;* Philip Cousineau's *The Art of Pilgrimage;* the Russian tale *The Way of a Pilgrim;* Tom Wright's *The Way of the Lord;* Patricia Hampl's *Virgin Times;* David Lodge's *Therapy;* Bruce Feiler's *Walking the Bible;* Rebecca West's train ride through parts of Europe I know little about in

Black Lamb and Grey Falcon; the American version of pilgrimage in Jack Kerouac's *On the Road,* stories of people visiting Elvis's tomb at Graceland, Tennessee, on the twenty-fifth anniversary of his death — to name but a few books, authors, and events.

I watch movies that promise a journey, even remotely, like *Central Station, Thelma and Louise, Dark City, O Brother, Where Art Thou? White Squall, Antonia's Line,* and *Chocolat.* On television, I am captivated by the exotic, romantic, and faraway locales of the Travel Channel and eye-opening images on the National Geographic channel, along with sweet and gentle Rick Steve's risk-free middle-class adventures in Europe, shown on the local PBS station at bizarre times of the night or early morning.

I am most captivated by the stories of other pilgrims and the memories they evoke within me. Their stories make me feel most sane when I feel the tug toward the craziness of life as we share stories of encountering the Holy in near locales or faraway lands, distant times as well as relatively recent moments, among friends or with strangers we don't know. Their stories give a romantic patina to the quirky, ancient practice of pilgrimage, which gives me the name of "pilgrim." Pilgrimage is not so much about human intention or invention, for it is not a time of sightseeing and relaxation, but a time of conversion. Pilgrimage is a God-induced time, a *kairos* moment. Pilgrimage is a period of companionship with Christ as our accompanier. The path before us reveals itself each step of the way, faith blazing the trail before us. Suddenly, amid the busyness of life there is an opening space on our crowded schedule, or we feel the need to sweep away all that is before us in order to make time a blessed time, in which we find ourselves on the road again, pulled by our noses by the Holy Spirit. Rather than being a great mistake that forces people on the road, this is a mystical divine invitation to come and follow Christ in our world today, making the follower a dangerous person to others who have resisted and denied the call and stayed at home.

In one book on the history of pilgrimage, I was smitten with the simple medieval woodcut image of the wayfaring pilgrim, sporting a simple necklace with a scallop shell over his tunic, leaning on a wooden staff, wearing a broad-brimmed hat and leather sandals. Today, the outfit would consist of sunglasses, backpack, water bottle, T-shirt, shorts, and Birkenstocks or lightweight hiking boots. Indeed, *becoming* a pilgrim is like putting on clothes that announce that one *is* a pilgrim. I'm still uncomfortable and restless. Sunday school classes, youth group lock-ins, and college campus devotions did not prepare me. The clothes of the pilgrim are too large for me, too baggy. There is no smooth "hand in glove" fit. I have to grow into the clothes of the pilgrimage. It is like my checking my nine-year-old son's new shoes to feel if there is "room to grow." It is like what Paul says: put on the Lord Jesus Christ.

My intellectual curiosity about pilgrimage was growing at the same time that I was experiencing a great personal struggle, in which I set off on a personal pilgrimage. I would learn later on, in retrospect, that the intellectual study of pilgrimage gave me the knowledge of other people's experiences and the words that would make my personal pilgrimage more comprehensible and realizable. This struggle had to do with an unexpected turn in the domestic pathway set before me years before. Dante writes in his first lines of the *Divine Comedy*: "I came to myself within a dark wood where the straight way was lost." Indeed, darkness became like day to me, so frequent a visitor was it in my life.

The "straight way" or highway was my marriage to a wonderful person, both of us in our early twenties and living out the middle-class American dreamscape presented to us by our family histories, museums, schools, literature, film, television, storefronts, banks, the U.S. government, Broadway musicals, and, of course, the church. Together we undertook a journey that was to last a lifetime. Each milestone was clearly marked and provided for, thanks to the surrounding American culture that promised us the great American marriage if we stuck wholeheartedly and with no questions asked to the pathway set before us. It was all quite easy: get married in your early twenties, have babies in your thirties, hit peak economic conditions in your forties as a professor at a major divinity school, attend the college graduations of your children in your fifties, and enjoy sweet retirement in your sixties, with the promise of grandchildren in the aging seventies. It was so easy in its preplanned sort of way: an AAA Trip-Tik with the orange highlighting pen showing us the way on the interstate highways — with none of the red state highways or blue highways marked. We got into our station wagon — big enough for at least a family of four — and sped on our way, singing "Beyond the blue horizon."

After twenty-one years of marriage, with marriage and family on cruise-control in our family-laden station wagon, zooming along at a fast, comfortable speed, filled with remarkable memories — from great adventures here and abroad, graduate schools for both of us, the incredible celebration of childbirth twice in our lives, and a year living in England — I suddenly turned off the interstate we were both on and came to an abrupt halt. There were anomalous "things" about the relationship, about me, that I could no longer live with, but couldn't — or wouldn't — name,

48

for fear that I would be rejected from the American dream script, replaced by someone more handsome and intelligent and creative.

The marriage entered a time of doubt, unease, unhappiness, suspicion, and more doubt and confusion. The car didn't work as well anymore. We looked at maps together to see where we were, and then started looking at different maps, at diverging roads, separately. I kept stopping the car of marriage, not able to go much further, slowly raising doubts about my place in the marriage, in the car, on the road.

An image: On long trips, I like doing the driving. There is something about getting in the car and going somewhere that I find intoxicating. In my family it was assumed I would be the first to drive. Where were we in the marriage? I was getting into a different car and driving, leaving behind the family car, literally and figuratively.

Once I got out of the family car, out of the marriage, and started driving my own car, stopping to walk on a different road that was stretching before me, I came to see that it was not a road intended for us. I entered a time of legal and physical separation from the person to whom I said, "I do" years before in a fairy-tale wedding in our home church. Our separation from one another had come after years of countless therapy sessions, both together and individually, and nights of trying to figure out how to stay together yet living honestly with who we are and our diverging hopes and dreams for the future. What made it possible for us to talk through all the years of separating from the commitments that bound us together was and is our love and fondness for each other. Yet knowing each other's strengths and abilities, we also knew too well each other's Achilles' heel and

49

would strike out whenever we wanted the undivided attention of the other. In one week's time, we could go through moments of great camaraderie and yet be at our wit's end wondering how we could civilly live under the same roof one more night.

To continue the metaphor, I got out of the car in which we were riding as a family only a few years ago. In the cold month of January, before this New Mexican pilgrimage in hot June, I had dinner with the family I had known for many years, in the house I called home for over six years, and then left with a friend for a concert of Phillip Glass music. Quietly, without fanfare, I had moved some of my clothes, some simple furnishings, dinnerwear, bed linens and towels to a studio apartment in Chapel Hill. It was a cold night, shivering cold. I was never to return to the house that had been home again. That night, I went to the studio apartment I had leased, and drank a glass of vodka with my friend in the dark quiet of the night.

It was a dark night in a dark forest.

Earlier in the month, a friend who is also a minister met with us one evening. She had us read aloud to one another the marriage vows, wanting us to listen and remember what we were breaking in our separation and subsequent divorce. While the actual divorce didn't occur for another two years, this was the night that the relationship, the covenant of marriage, changed forever. I felt empty and cold that evening as I wrote down for my former spouse and the minister my feelings about what I was breaking: something sacred and whole was being shattered in front of me, in my very hands, and there was nothing I could do to prevent its destruction. Tears could no longer come forth from dry eyes and a wounded heart. All I could remember was a deep, dark pit of emptiness in the place where the heart of the marriage once beat strong. An eerie quiet took its place.

That night was the beginning of a pilgrimage that I came to understand only because of the pilgrimage in New Mexico: it started quietly and understated, as it was the dying of a "Once upon a time" fairy-tale wedding and marriage.

If I was leaving a marriage, then what was I entering into? Only then emerging, in the barrenness of my life, was an amazing new sense of whose I am. Gone were some of the small and large falsehoods or masks or costumes or even the desire to play hide-and-go-seek with others or myself anymore. God's grace is neither starry light nor soft pealing church bells: God's grace is ear-splitting thunderclap as I am cracked open wide, my being exposed for all the lies and deceits I have tried to maintain, shattering the thin veneer of my well-protected being and pretentious self. Over the next few dusty miles of this pilgrimage I would learn to identify and leave behind the excess baggage of heightened expectation of others for my life. This was a vital move in order to open, and sometimes fight to remain open, to the mystery of God in my life, and of life in God, in the body of Christ, that is always unfolding before me and revealing itself around me.

Leaving behind parts of the fabricated, fairytale, false identity of who I am, or was, I entered this pilgrimage of unexpected severe beauty of life around me, and with increasing curiosity, hopeful anticipation, and edgy wariness (or is it exhaustion?) regarding the miracle to be found at El Santuario de Chimayo. This trek to Chimayo would be the first step, a starting point, a distinct place of departure. The broken relationship that I caused, with great suffering on the part of my former wife, yet my continuing to be a father of two beautiful children, propels me to move toward something or someone. Where to? Could it be a holy place, like Chimayo, wherein lies Gilead's promised balm of healing power? Could it be the chance of a lifetime to meditate along arid stretches of New Mexican land, reflecting the arid desert within me? Or could it be discovering a host of motley pilgrims, strangers to me but not one another, who would come to accept me for who I am within a week, holding me closer to myself and God as I remain stumped by the riddle of my complex and knotted life?

I am outside the house where Kit Carson slept in downtown Taos. Among many of the people in Taos Pueblo, Kit Carson is seen as the enemy of the people, a conqueror. I find a phone booth and call North Carolina to talk with my children once more before I leave the life I knew behind. Tears well up in my eyes. The children sound happy and are eager to get back to what they were doing in North Carolina.

Day One: The Rituals That Bind Us Together

At 1:00 p.m., Father Ed and I drive north to sparsely populated Costilla on the border of southern Colorado and northern New Mexico. We park Father Ed's car in the empty, dusty parking lot of Costilla Elementary School and are soon joined by several minivans, some cars, and a few pickup trucks. Fathers and mothers, young boys and siblings of all ages disembark and unpack their vehicles of sleeping bags and duffel bags while mothers and daughters mill around. Some parents are nervous for their children, while some mothers have an urgent desire to get back to a busy schedule and a week's holiday from their beloved children and husbands.

I learned the rituals of this pilgrimage by immersion in them, or as they say in the South, "baptism by fire." Before the evening meal I was inaugurated into new rituals that would begin to bind this gathering of straggling individuals into a more unified band of pilgrims. The first ritual or routine began with the simple shout of "Formation!" by the director or lead pilgrim. When we heard "Formation" bellowed, we were to get into a single file behind three standards: the *guía* (meaning guide), a wooden cross with the corpus on it that was to be our guide; a flag with the imprint of our Lady of Guadalupe (a.k.a. Mother Mary of the Americas), followed by a large wooden puzzle piece that was part of the heart of Jesus.

I am transfixed by the northern New Mexican corpus, as the representation of Jesus is radically different from anything I know of in my Protestant upbringing. It is alien to my middle-class American life. Jesus' head is bent down, his chin touching his chest, while his mouth is wide open as if he is screaming in pain. A crown of thorns is placed firmly upon his head, causing a profusion of blood to cascade from his brow and over his entire body. The hands and feet are frozen in a spasm of pain as the nails go through them.

Once in single file, we walk slowly to the small Catholic church in Costilla and perform another ritual to be repeated often throughout this journey: as we come close to the church, singing a simple song — usually in Spanish — members of the church are singing another song, carrying in front of them a large banner with an image of the patron saint of the church on it in bright colors and impressive detail. Along this pilgrimage we will see banners of St. Anthony of Padua, St. Joseph, St. Jerome, St. Teresa of Jesus, and Our Lady. Once the pilgrims holding the *guía* and the church members meet, the singing continues or ceases while the pilgrims kiss and venerate the *guía* we are carrying and the banner of the church we are visiting. The church members, including the priest, lead the way into the church, and we follow in single file and quiet.

Right before the entrance of the church, there is another curious, mystical encounter: parishioners line up and create a corridor, which we pass through. They reach out and touch us gently with their hands, smiling and asking for a blessing. An older woman touches my hand and raises it to her weathered, aged, wrinkled forehead in order for me to give her a blessing. I am told that in the eyes of some parishioners, we are considered specially blessed by God because of the sacrifice of time and energy we are making this week; in the eyes of some parishioners, we are saints, treated as royalty, "a chosen race . . . God's own people" (1 Pet. 2:9). Slips of papers with prayer requests are stuffed into our hands, to be taken to holy Chimayo, but also prayed for during the week. We are in the process of becoming *peregrinos*, pilgrims of God.

Other rituals small and large, meaningful and quirky, if not downright arcane, act like twine that binds this loose conglomeration of individuals into an increasingly closer band of pilgrims. Such small rituals include the act of relieving oneself on the roadside — don't run before the *guía* — and always following the *guía* into every place we go, whether a church, a dining hall, or the next elementary school gym.

Sometimes the rituals provide a built-in rest stop, like praying the Angelus at 6:00 a.m. and 6:00 p.m., repeating "Hail Mary, full of grace, the Lord is with you."

One small ritual that was full of meaning was doffing one's baseball hat before a church, a cemetery, or a roadside cross as a sign of reverence. At first, we only doffed our hats at Catholic sites, but within the week, we were doffing them in front of Protestant churches as well, no matter how big or small. I called it a "Protestant moment" in this Catholic monoculture.

One of the richest rituals performed during the week was the blessing of food. At the end of our meal, the men on pilgrimage and the Guadalupanas — the women who supported us on this pilgrimage — would gather together to receive a blessing from us. It would begin with one of the pilgrims thanking the cooks for a delicious meal, followed by our singing, in chorus, "May the blessings of God be upon you," with our hands raised up as a sign of blessing. Then we would get down on one knee and the cooks would pray a blessing for us, singing the same song while holding out their hands, palms down. Then, before leaving the vicinity, we would gather slips of paper with prayers written on them and take a pinch of soil from the place, to be delivered up to God at Chimayo.

Slowly I introduced myself to the other pilgrims, many of whom knew each other from other pilgrimages. They are now veterans. We continue to talk into the evening as we gather sleeping bags and pads together, encircling the *guía*, which is placed on a quilt composed of the various T-shirt designs from past pilgrimages. This first night we are given the Prayer of Abandonment by Brother Charles of Jesus to pray and meditate upon as a group:

> Father, I abandon myself into your hands;
> Do with me what you will.
> Whatever you may do, I thank you:
> I am ready for all, I accept all....
> Into your hands I commend my soul.

All is still and quiet, the words of the prayer searching and probing our lives in a stealthy manner. Father Ed asks for us to consider prayerfully which words are the hardest or easiest to pray. Then the good Father asks a haunting question: "Imagine Jesus praying this prayer to you!" This question begins to crawl under my skin and spread through my entire being; it burrows itself in unpleasant places in my life. Having just left North Carolina and the responsibility for moving out of a marriage, the last thing I wanted was the odious charge of being responsible for the life of Jesus. Into the shadows of life the light of Christ begins to shine as this question nudges awake the guilt, the faith, the insecurities, the obstacles, the sense of unworthiness deep within. Jesus? Pray this prayer to me, as if I could be of aid? Jesus doesn't want such a wounded, broken person like me to help. I need Jesus' holiness to be the balm of healing for my tragic sense of guilt. Miraculously, I fall asleep with only these vital, uneasy questions swirling and churning deep within me, unanswerable and opening me up for a week of questioning life.

Day Two: The Community of the Foot

We were aroused at three o'clock in the morning. The night was filled with the shuffling of men's feet across the old dusty gym floor, with the floor creaking in response to the stumbling footsteps. In the middle of the night, a thirteen-year-old boy shouts for his mother. Meanwhile, the snoring men labor onward. I miss my soft yet firm pillow and hard mattress with the downy liner in North Carolina. I miss the quietness of the night. I miss the air conditioner as I throw off the top of my sleeping bag.

Yesterday was a day of gathering pilgrims and beginning the spiritual and intellectual pilgrimage. Today we move onward, putting into play the physical pilgrimage. Lining up outside the quaint antique gym of Costilla School we form a loose single-file line: the *guía* before us, the flag of our Lady, the heart of Jesus, and the strand of pilgrims, followed up by pickup trucks, one holding a large water container, and the other holding our gear. "It is four in the morning," I repeat to myself. Without so much as an "On your mark, get set, go," we begin the pilgrimage. I was starting to fall asleep on my feet in the back of the line when we began. A kind nudge by Deacon Don in the back of the line gets me moving. His walking stick is an old ski pole, minus the rubber cuff. The "click, click, click" keeps me moving forward, for fear that I will be stabbed at any moment.

I know that in North Carolina everyone is sound asleep in their beds. "This pilgrimage is crazy," I say to myself.

We walk out of the area where a few streetlights shine, into the yawning audible silence of the night. No wind, no sound but the scuffling of running shoes and hiking boots upon the crumbling, sandy shoulder of the roadway. No birds fly or call to another at this hour, but bats wing frantically and silently, swooping near our heads. A large old moose ambles by, crossing the strip of road before us, ignoring us completely. The *guía* is before us, Colorado's majestic, rugged white-tipped snow cone mountains behind us. The jagged outline of a vast tree-covered mountain range is on our left, covered in a black drape, while the sprawling desert on our right looks like a gray tarpaulin, stretching thousand of acres over arid wasteland. The black-satin morning sky is cluttered with flickering stars, squeezing in to make their presence known, while the crescent moon resembles an overripe slice of cantaloupe as it hangs over our heads.

I didn't know that it would it become cooler by the minute as we walk into the dark vale toward the brightness of the morning. It is downright chilly in the early June morning.

Down the road a bit we traipse by two horses in a corral. They stare at our undulating line, which must look like an enormous slithering, threatening black snake to them. They are greatly disturbed by our slouching presence, their smooth brown muscular bodies rigid, every limb of their bodies tense. Their eyes grow larger. Frightened, they explode and release their pent-up anxiety, galloping fiercely away to the opposite end of the corral, turn, and then charge back at us, staring intently and yet guardedly as they come up to the snaky line of pilgrims. Meanwhile, the cows on our right chew their cud quietly.

Having walked three hours, stopping only to pray the Angelus at six in the morning, we stop on a dusty side road to check our feet. This is the first time I consider the bodily education of being a pilgrim and the physical toll of being on pilgrimage. We sit down, take off shoes and socks, and start the inspection: slightly red spots on the feet get moleskin; raised red or bubbles on the skin get lanced as they are blisters. Blisters are found on people's heels, the balls of feet, between toes, and anywhere that skin rubs against skin. For some, knees are aching, and Ace bandages are applied. Others complain of ingrown toenails. Yards of moleskin patches are cut in weird shapes to fit the aching foot. "Pass the scissors," and "more foot powder needed here" are messages heard above the cutting of moleskin and the pleasing sighs evoked by the massaging of muscles.

My jet-flying, station-wagoned existence in North Carolina is challenged on this very first day. Wendell Berry writes that we are able to process information at about the pace of walking, for that is the primary way of transporting ourselves. Even when we jog or run we miss some of the intricacies of the environment around us, or a small sound that is distinctive yet quiet. Bikes move us quicker, a car even faster, and a jet lets us get a bird's-eye view of the world, but we miss the finer details of life below us and around us.

This day is given to discovering the community that emerges — miraculously — around the ordinary foot. Contrary to what St. Paul says about the foot in his pictorial narrative about the body of Christ — hand versus foot — the foot reigned mighty and supreme over any other part of our bodies on this pilgrimage, served by the mind and spirit (1 Cor. 12). There were times that I could not take one more step from sheer exhaustion, yet I told myself "One more step," felt the surge of the will come to the fore, and the steps soon followed.

Some days we would sing songs with a military-like cadence to get us to walk in rhythm. I expected us to sing "Over hill, over dale, we will hit the dusty trail. . . . " Other days, we sang lilting verses of the Gospel in Spanish, or chanted prayers aloud, walking to the downbeat of the chant. On one day of the pilgrimage, one of the silver-haired *peregrinos* began to sing and then holler: "Draw on Jesus Christ, crucified and resurrectified as the medicine for what ails ya!" Jesus as the medicine of *life!*

Along the roadside, in the chapels, and every evening in the gyms and armories where we stayed, the places were transformed into an infirmary for our wounded, broken, tired feet. Yes, my legs and arms, back and shoulders, would also wince in muscle aches and spasms, but nothing compared to the upkeep of the lowly, the smelly, the mundane foot.

Where I saw the Spirit sowing seeds of community was in the gestures of young men who became medics, massaging the older men's feet, thighs, knees, and calves. The sweet smell of Bengay mingling with witch hazel ointment and other home remedies from the roots of trees permeated entire gyms. The young men — seventeen or eighteen years old — would wash down the purple varicose-veined legs of older men with rubbing alcohol. Or they would take the yellowish, gnarled, fungus covered foot of a middle-aged man, placing the foot in his lap and massaging each toe with tender care. The young medics would look the one being cared for in the eye and speak encouraging words about being a pilgrim. They would look at the wound without wincing, but with compassion. One of the leaders of the pilgrimage boasted of his white-headed blister within the larger red, now infected blister on the sole of his right foot. I looked at the bottom of his feet and cringed, feeling the pain of the other.

What was so captivating and brought community to life was the intimacy, a gentle care displayed in such simple healing gestures among these men, between young and old, found only in these unrecoverable moments of vulnerable suffering in the presence of another. On the first day many of us shook hands with perfect strangers, struggling to remember a person's name and hometown. With the elements of foot powder and bandages, touching each other's feet as we stare in each other's eyes, learning stories about each other's schools and families, we move from an aggregation of individuals to resemble a community of pilgrims. The seeds of Christian community are sown in the application of needles to blisters and talcum powder to feet. Moleskin scraps dotted with wet gels are applied to the hot soles of our feet. Miraculous ointments are spread on knee joints and sprained ankles. As Jesus took the wash basin and towel to wash his disciples' feet, we too become Christ's hands, participating anew in this ancient ritual's healing processes.

Day Three: "He Ain't on the Cross Anymore!"

We sleep in Questa tonight, awaking at three o'clock in the morning and on the road by four... again. Yesterday was "baptism by fire" into the physicality of pilgrimage. Today, my spirit and mind join the physical pilgrimage as I sense I am over one hurdle in the education of being a pilgrim. We walk out of the artificial glow of streetlights in sleeping Questa, into the dark maw of the cold night before us.

We stop by a roadside crucifix: a three-foot white plastic cross tilting slightly to the left. It is still festooned with a collection of plastic flowers, now a faded relic of memories. What was once a bright, bouncy bouquet of Mylar balloons is now shredded, whipping in the chilly morning breeze. A young boy's name is crudely printed with black marking pen on the cross, with his birthday and the day of his death underneath his name. One of the *peregrinos* whispers to me, "He was hit by a drunk driver, right on this spot. Our hats come off, we pray the *Sudario,* a prayer for his soul.

At 7:30, the vehicle traffic increases dramatically. Suddenly, without warning, an old man, white haired, an angry scowl on his craggy face, slows down in his 1980 white Oldsmobile Cutlass sedan. He rolls down the window on the passenger side, his left hand shooting toward us violently as he points with his gnarled finger toward the Christ on the cross. He leans toward us and yells accusingly, "He ain't on the cross anymore!" He jerks his head, his body, inside after rolling up the passenger side window. He guns his engine, leaving a smoky trail behind him, as if he were afraid we would run after him as a group, catch him, and beat him up with the cross of Christ and the flag of Our Lady, leaving him at the side of the road near the empty Oldsmobile sedan.

All of our heads turned to the insulting driver; we stared blankly, our mouths open wide as we swallowed the evil epithets hurled at us. In retrospect, his words were like a Molotov cocktail just freshly lit in an *old* beer bottle. After the stunned silence wore off we began to talk among ourselves, even though we were instructed to be in silent devotion for this portion of the pilgrimage. "What did he say?" "Did he say what I *think* he said?" said some of the younger pilgrims.

As the lone Protestant, a minister, and an educator of Christians professionally, I couldn't believe what just happened. As a white male in Protestant America, I never get yelled at on the roadways or sidewalks of North Carolina. But in this crowd I was no longer a white Protestant from North Carolina, but one of the brown Catholics of New Mexico. I am dumbfounded by the vitriol of the driver. Such anti-Catholic sentiments are foreign to me. Clearly the driver of the sedan is a Protestant, like me, perhaps an evangelical. Yet amid my Catholic, Spanish-speaking brothers, I am one of them.

I can't imagine what it would be like to be yelled at with such hate, day in and day out. I think of those African Americans, sitting at a counter in a department store in Greensboro, North Carolina, and the abuse they suffered. I think of those women chained to fences in their support of the ERA Amendment. I think of those who berated Cesar Chavez in his quest for farmworker rights. I think of those who taunt young gay youth at Pride parades in small southern towns — "Fag," "Fairy" — and the Fred Phelps followers who jeer at gays and lesbians in those states in which equality for all is the watchword for the movement.

The discussion that then took place was better than any Sunday school or youth group coffee klatch that I have ever been part of in my life. Deeply serious theological discussions took place, and quickly, right there on the roadside. On the one hand, I am told that many Catholics can't seem to get past Good Friday and worship a Jesus who is risen from the dead. On the other hand, many of the Protestants I worship with tend to forget that Jesus was ever on the cross before he arose from the dead: a resurrection with no sacrificial death. This man's epithet became a moment of genuine education: who *is* the God we worship in our churches with no Christ on the cross? Do Protestants have sacraments? How many? When do we baptize? Do you have wine when you have Eucharist? What? You don't call it Eucharist? What *do* you call it then?

Drivers and riders in air-conditioned cars and minivans, semi-trucks, SUVs, and large mobile homes drive by us, honk at us, give us "thumbs-up" signs. We walk onward, walking for others, including the angry man, carrying the needs and concerns of others and ourselves to a place called Chimayo.

Day Four: Searching Sanctuaries

We slept in the National Guard Armory last night: it was cleaner than the places we had slept the last two nights. And we received the gift of being able to sleep late: six o'clock this morning is when we were aroused by the piercing sound of a gym instructor's whistle.

Outside the Armory, Father Ed brought us to a patch of earth that was largely void of prairie grass, where we formed a large circle, overlooking Taos. Father Ed reminded us that the earth is the Lord's, a belief that our ancestors held firmly, as did those people who lived and farmed and cared for this land before there were European settlers. He then dropped a leather pouch of tobacco upon the earth as a gift to the soil. With a clay bowl full of water, he blessed the earth as God's good creation, sprinkling the brown-red soil, leaving dimpled marks upon the dusty terrain. He placed the bowl in the center of our circle, and with his right hand he scooped out some water from the bowl and wetted his large body: first he touched the areas of his body that included the five senses; then he wet his limbs, one by one; finally he drew a ladle of water from the bowl and drank some of the water. Each one of us partook in the same ritual, with Father Ed giving us the ladle of water at the end of our soaking, concluding with this prayer: The earth is the Lord's, and all who inhabit it. Thanks be to God."

My Protestant heritage was feeling sterile. Never before had I partaken in such a ritual of thanks and honor of God for this incredible gift of this good creation. Much of my upbringing, as a Protestant and educator of Christians, had to do with the community of *people* before me and God above me, leaving behind in the creeds and confessions the place and presence of saints, let alone the land, or the wonder of candles, icons, and *Santos*. The words of the psalmist, filled to the brim with allusions to the land around us, are coming to life in extraordinary ways. "The earth is the Lord's, and all the fullness therein," writes the psalmist.

We leave behind the days of walking twenty miles or more to take a day for visiting chapels, sanctuaries, and churches in the Taos area. Being raised in the northern part of America, I have come to envision the church building as a white, wood-sided, neat, clean, and trim New England Congregational church, or as a colonial, Georgian, red brick and tall white-steepled church with large white pillars of North Carolina, or as an urban fortress a faux-Gothic cathedral with a fieldstone facades, numerous steps to get inside, and gorgeous, intricate Tiffany-like stain-glass windows.

But in Taos, many of the sanctuaries we visited this day seemed to be rising from the very soil upon which they were founded. Many were as red-brown as the earth they sat upon. Others were the very definition of beige, tanned from the bleaching effects of the sun. The walls almost looked like the color of cappuccino.

These churches sat fat upon the land, the base of the church being broader than the upper portions of the church structure. These churches felt like they were made by human hands and not the professional clean hands of an architectural firm faraway. These churches had the feeling that they housed God's people in all their roughness, readiness, brokenness, fragility, and toughness.

There are almost no square angles on these churches; everything is a little bit off kilter as they are made not only by imperfect human hands, but of rough timbers, as well as straw and clay-like mud. Outside one sanctuary in Ranchos de Taos, they are fixing the walls with clay-like mud in wheelbarrows, and everyone's hands drip with the earthen lumps and liquid. I liked going up to the side of these sanctuaries, to feel the sensual yet rough-to-the-touch walls. On the outside, the sun's rays warmed and baked the earthen structures, but inside, the walls were cool as the ecru white paint that covered the walls.

The white of the walls provided a marvelous canvas. In many sanctuaries in the north, if one were to spread colored paint on the wall with a design, or smear finger paints, or use chalk and crayons, the vestry or elders would convene a meeting for discussion of the great atrocity before them. But in these sanctuaries, the people painted flowers of the region on the walls . . . in full bloom no less.

What also helps to cool these inner sanctuaries from the ravages of the sun in northern New Mexico is the very building material of these adobe structures: the prairie grass and mud plied on, layer by layer, with a bare framework of rough wooden timber, with many new layers of mud and grass to repair the walls, acting as nature's own insulation. The bare-beamed ceiling and light pine wooden floors add a sense of rustic beauty to these marvelous structures. In one sanctuary, in Truchas — built in 1776 — I was told by a member of the congregation that many priests are buried beneath the wooden floors. Why? Because they believed that if you were buried close to the altar in the sanctuary, you would be among the first to be redeemed on the coming day of glory. I didn't bother to ask what it meant to be buried out in the church's graveyard, further away from the sanctuary's altar.

All of this was alien to my Protestant sensibilities. The Presbyterians of the North and Southeast where I lived believed strongly in the scriptural mantra of doing everything "decently and in order," a line that St. Paul should always regret uttering, for it gives scriptural permission for a certain kind of obsessiveness and control in church architecture.

I laughed when I entered the parish of St. Anthony in Cordova, the sanctuary filled from floor to ceiling with *Santos*. *Santos* are those icons, candles, and small statues of Jesus, the Virgin Mary, Peter, Paul, St. Anthony, Our Lady of Guadalupe, St. Benedict, St. Joseph, St. Francis de Sales, and others. Statues of various sizes and postures with hands folded in prayer lined a shelf built in to the adobe wall of the sanctuary. This is rare, if only because for some years now *Santos* have been stolen from parishes in this area, showing up as museum pieces and antique relics in antique stores in Soho and Chelsea in New York City and some in L.A. My favorite *Santos* in this church are on an enormous wooden screen both in front and on the side of the sanctuary. An image of Jesus and St. Francis appear together in one painting, along with the symbol of St. Francis's black-robed arm crossing the arm of the wounded Jesus.

On this evening we visited a *morada,* or small chapel, of the *Hermanos* of the Rancho de Taos area, for a dinner of hot dogs and hamburgers. The *Hermanos* — otherwise known as the Brothers of the *Pentitentes* — began in Spain and spread over to the States as a lay society of men whose chief purpose since the eighteenth century has been the burial of people from Spain or countries south of the North American border. There are married and unmarried men who lead a life of devotion to Christ.

When we entered their property we were greeted by a small band of *Hermanos* singing a mournful, wailing song, walking behind their smaller *guía.* We journeyed through their cemetery in the back of their *morada,* venerating the large cross at the far end of the property by either kissing the cross, kneeling in front of it, or touching the cross with our finger tips and then performing the sign of the cross. We followed the small band of troubadours out of the cemetery and into a backyard enclosure, clouded by smoke from the grill and lifted up by the smell of barbecued hot dogs and hamburgers.

I wandered alone into the one-story sanctuary of their *morada.* All was dark at first, as there was no electricity in the building. As my eyes adjusted to the lack of light, I encountered a larger-than-life statue of Jesus, looking eerily like one of Alberto Giacometti's statues. This wooden, al-most anorexic Jesus was dressed in a red burlap alb, a large crown of thorns on his oversized head, which was causing great bleeding. This Jesus' hands were also larger than life, way out of proportion with the rest of his thin, wraith-like body. His palms were open to the viewer, held out to show where the nails tore away the flesh from the hands, and his feet were cut deeply by nails as long and thick as railroad spikes. Far smaller than this looming Jesus was a statue of Mary, accompanying this agonizing Christ, her head bent in deep sorrow from the horror of it all, with other even smaller statuettes surrounding this assemblage. The flicker-ing votive candles were the only source of light, casting an eerie, ethereal glow around the crucified Christ. One *pere-grino* quietly told me that when the *Hermanos* bury their dead, it is a replay of Good Friday . . . with no hope of Easter.

The mixture of the vision of death with the savory smell of grilled meat outside caught me off balance. The country-club churches where I grew up as a young boy and adolescent, with physical structures that looked like they belonged *at* the country club, and with a crowd who were dues-paying members of the country clubs, dressed in Polo shirts and khaki slacks, celebrated a faith in which there was no cost for salvation. It was a sanitized faith, with grace washing my hands so that the germ of sin would not be found on my lily-white skin. The absence of any Christ on a cross was at odds with the grisly human drama por-trayed in such pitiful, moving graphic detail in places like this *morada*. On this pilgrimage I was slowly being educated into an inescapable human dimension of the faith that I had been able to either avoid like a bad plague, or ward off all these years while living in pleasant places.

Day Five: It's the Land, Stupid!

The morning wake-up call was early again: three o'clock! I've got my morning preparations down to a ritual: I begin by slathering my white face, ears, the back of my neck, and my arms and legs with creamy white sun block: SPF 45! I then put on my white T-shirt and apply a thick layer of petroleum jelly wherever skin will rub. I take the anti–athlete's foot cream and smear it between, over, and under my toes and the soles of my feet. I finish up by carefully sticking the moleskin over oozing gel pads. I lace and re-lace my walking shoes so that the shoe is one with the foot. At four-thirty we were on a long, dark, winding road, entering Carson National Park.

The first road is called the "U.S." highway. This name was given not out of patriotic pride, but the shape of the road: we make a big U, followed by a winding S pattern. I am awakened from this road tour by a brilliant white stream of light bursting forth from the nearby military base: a rocket shoots forward into the stillness of white stars and crescent moon. All that is left from this bright, fiery announcement is a gentle mist of gaseous substance, which dissipates into nothingness. A brother pilgrim comes up behind me and tells me that Roswell, New Mexico, is over a certain hill: "Aliens" he whispers, and then laughs out loud during our time of silent prayer.

I then turn around, right before we enter the forest, and see spread before me Taos and vicinity, set against a mountainside, looking like sparkling diamonds placed upon a jeweler's black velvet cloth. The relative quiet of people not talking makes more profound the sounds of nature this early morning: chirping crickets, howling wild dogs, scurrying chipmunks, the flapping of a bat's wings, and the falcon gliding on a whisper "whoosh" of wind.

In North Carolina, I am surrounded by the green of forest, placed in prominent places for privacy in the suburbs of Chapel Hill, and the green grass carpet of lawns. The pine corridors of roads and the kudzu vines smothering the life of trees are overpowering in its greenness. The kudzu looks like shabby upholstery over the remains of trees the vine has killed off.

Likewise, in North Carolina, I had stopped breathing. The "conditions" around my separation and upcoming divorce had stopped me from breathing. I was holding my breath, scared of when I would hear a rumor spread by my distant wife. To create community, she would often tell others why we were separating and divorcing. While I understood and tried to explain to her and others the complex and changing reasons for why I was leaving the marriage, but not leaving the role of father, my separated Other would tell people *her* version. I found out, years later, that telling one's story first, especially if it is a story of victimhood, is a way of creating a community quickly. Scared of what she was telling others, rightly or wrongly, I had stopped breathing and was holding my breath from the fear of not knowing what was going to happen next. Perhaps if I were silent — an impossibility for me — I could carry on with life as usual.

The complexities of my inner life found an amazing congruity and fit with the life and geography of northern New Mexico. I felt strangely at home in the vast sweep of desert land, interrupted by the verdant *arroyos* — magnificent rock-striated chasms scarring the otherwise flat parched desert land with water — and bounteous deciduous trees teeming with crawling life.

I am holding the *guía* as we walk up the mountain. As I look *through* the *guía*, I see the crucified Christ, whose arms are outstretched, embracing the surrounding land: the jagged mountains topped with white snow that looks like ice cream it's so pure, with the base of scruffy pine trees amid soaring evergreen trees with brown underbrush; the dawdling porcupine; the hungry eagle soaring overhead on the whispering air; a pair of bicyclists stopping to talk with us: all of this is part of God's creation. This land throbs with life, pulsating with a current of energy, set tick-tocking by the Maker's hands. The rhythm of life, of birth, the living and the dead, season following season, swiftly changing weather patterns, all make for the slightly nuanced and intricate texture of God's land, which breaks open into bounteous vistas, more fantastic than the mind's eye can take in. We pray this morning: "With beauty before me, may I walk; with beauty behind me, may I walk ... wandering on a trail of beauty, *lively* I walk," — stressing lively with glee. Georgia O'Keeffe was astute in her observation that Christianity is like a veil over this land as Christ's Spirit permeates all that was, that is, and that ever shall be. While the Catholic Church may have been here for four hundred years, God was present way before the church, infusing the land with life before the people came to rest and walk and build and plant upon the soil. This is *holy ground.*

Georgia O'Keeffe found her peace in this land, as did the tuberculosis-ridden soul of D. H. Lawrence. The story was told to me that after his death overseas, Lawrence's ashes arrived in Taos. They took his ashes up to a mesa, and before they could ceremoniously spread the ashes, a great gust of wind took the ashes and lifted them up into the horizon and spread them upon God's creation.

The scenery is so great, so wide, so magnificent, that my problems in North Carolina seem appropriately small. It is on this pilgrimage that I now begin to realize that God is reaching out to me in my void of being, plucking my irascible soul and kicking body, and preserving my life from the ultimate pit of destruction. In separation and divorce, one can't help but wonder if one is on a path of self-destruction, coming undone by one's own hands, or if this stripping away of what is known is an act of God's cleansing, grace-inclined actions. This terrain is as dramatic and jagged to the touch as is my life. As I come to voluntarily — and involuntarily — break out of society's norms for my suburban existence, I am looking over vistas that make me see and feel and touch and smell God's genuine artistry in making all things brand-spanking new around me. As I settle down on a cliff side and watch the playful dance of sunlight and gray storm clouds pull out oranges and shades of pink from brown soil and hanging rocks, I can think of nothing more fantastic than what God has done in this land — and is doing in my life: "The living, the living give you thanks, as I do today, O Lord" writes the prophet Isaiah.

The Final Day: El Santuario de Chimayo, or Bust!

Chimayo is right around the bend and over a few hills, or so I am told. I am filled with conflicting thoughts and emotions; while I wish to see my friend Paul and soak in a pool for a day or two, I am sorry to see the time come to an end. We pilgrims, we *peregrinos,* are rapidly opening up our moribund, cocoon-like lives, becoming a community of pilgrims, of Christians, aching to be borne as we share intimately with one another the tender moments of our lives.

Chimayo is a magical, mystical place. The area of Chimayo was holy ground for the Tewa people, who lived in this land before the Spaniards arrived. The Tewa believed there was a sacred pool of mud, which cured people of their wounds, a place brought forth from fire and water. In 1810, Don Benardo Abeyta, a Spanish Catholic settler in this place — then a Mexican territory — was praying the Stations of the Cross along the hillside around Chimayo. He saw a light springing up from one of the hillside slopes. When he got close to it, he realized the light was coming from the ground itself. Digging with his hands to the source of the light he found a crucifix. He took the crucifix to the church in Santa Cruz nearby, but it was gone the next morning: it had returned to the spot where it was found. This happened two more times in the next few days. The people in this area decided to build a chapel at the spot. This chapel contains the very hole with its healing earth — *el pocito* — which has become the "Lourdes of the Americas." Many say that if you take soil from this hole for healing, it replenishes itself. This soil with its healing power is the miracle of Chimayo. Sadly, in more recent times it has also become a place of drug trafficking, resulting in many untimely deaths upon this sacred soil.

The day we pilgrims arrived was magnificent in many ways. To begin, there were five groups of pilgrims who were converging on Chimayo that day. The other groups also had thirty or more people, with two routes for women only, the other groups for men only, and they too had walked over one hundred miles. Next there was the euphoria of joyous embraces as old friends saw each other for the first time in a week. Husbands and wives, boy and girl friends, and other significant partners fell into each other's arms and wept openly. A mother races up the sanctuary's center aisle and catches her two-year-old daughter in a loving embrace. My friend Paul surprises me by embracing me from behind, and we hug warmly.

The pageantry of the final worship was non-stop; three Native American men pounded their native drums and sang us into worship. Each group's *guía* came and met the others in a circle joined by the colorful flags of Our Lady. The puzzle pieces of the heart of Jesus were put together in a large circle of soil that was made from all the bags of soil collected from the sites where we pilgrims stopped along the way. People shared stories from each pilgrimage route, telling of inclement weather, sprained ankles, and celebrations of the old and young among us. Sarah, a woman in her eighties, was the elder among us all. After Eucharist, Father Ed shouted to the pilgrims, *¡Qué Viva Cristo Rey!"* And we shouted back in unison for all the world to hear. The Native Americans began the call of the drums again, and slowly the company of pilgrims, of *peregrinos,* began to dissipate amid the task of finding our week-old gear, sleeping bags, and the loving arms of family and friends.

And yet the journey continues. The education of the pilgrim began with the body; it carves and embeds itself into my spirit and fills my every waking thought for the next few days, weeks, and now years. As I write this, I still remember vividly the people's faces, the sound of the drums, and dream of the wide open vistas. I pray the mealtime prayers, vowing to live for the benefit of all creation. I awaken singing pilgrimage songs — in Spanish no less. And wherever I drive by and see a roadside crucifix, I cross myself, taking off my hat before churches and walking carefully around horses.

On this pilgrimage I learned and am learning to live a life dependent less upon my own strategies and white-Anglo-Saxon-Protestant-male-middle-class wiles for success, but more and more upon the grace of God in Christ. It is not an easy lesson for me to learn. This is a lesson not learned in Sunday school or weekend seminars, or even weekend pilgrimage experiences. It is learned every day amid God's people, amid God's bounteous creation, through Christ, in the Holy Spirit. Through faith by grace, writes St. Paul, do we even have the initial energy, the consuming drive, the rousing desire to be swept up into the reign of God's fathomless love. Now I fall easily into the pool of God's grace, peace, and love, seeing in what ways each day is a pilgrimage, a journey, with the Holy Spirit...but will I remain this faithfully and romantically involved in another two weeks, months, or years? As a man in his forties, separated from his wife of twenty-plus years, yet a father, even amid the broken vows of marriage I began to see on this pilgrimage that God's faithfulness is ever abiding while my attention waivers. That is God's promise, the reason for hope, which carries me when I feel ensnared in the pain of my own making, unleashing the chaotic unknown upon my life: one day at a time, one step at a time, journeying onward, "to Chimayo."

As I get on the plane in Albuquerque, leaving my friend Paul and the raw sensations of pilgrimage, I leave to continue the pilgrimage that awaits me in Chapel Hill...for soon I will be moving into another significant relationship that has been waiting for me for some time now. The pilgrimage to Chimayo may have come to an end, but the awareness of life-as-pilgrimage has only begun....

Chapter Three

SIX MEN AND A CROSS

As I wrote earlier, it all began with that walk across the open highways of northern New Mexico, the only white, non-Spanish-speaking, Protestant "gringo" amid a straight line of shades of brown faces, on pilgrimage to the holy place of Chimayo, New Mexico. It is a hot June day, sweat trickling down my spine. My hat guards me from the hot sun shining directly overhead. But I walk on, for before me is a six-foot cross, with a northern New Mexican corpus of Christ hanging on it, highly venerated throughout this Catholic landscape.

My first inaugural pilgrimage was part of a larger annual pilgrimage, in which women and men walk over one hundred miles in six days, leaving from various parts of northern New Mexico to the small adobe church, El Santuario de Chimayo. It is there, in the small chapel, that one will find a round hole in holy soil — the *pocito* — that people come to touch, to taste, and to touch others in hopes of a miracle healing of mind, heart, or body.

The miracle for me was not in reaching Chimayo, though walking over one hundred miles in less than a week was a physically arduous yet spiritually and intellectually nurturing adventure. I came to know thirty-five other men as friends, men who were complete strangers to me at the beginning of the week. We all awoke at 3:00 in the morning, hitting the dusty roadside by 4:00, and walked until the early afternoon. By 10:00 in the evening, we all fell asleep in dusty gyms and Armory buildings along the trail. We prayed, sang, ate, laughed, listened, talked, prayed some more, and joked together for a fascinating week. The daily rituals of morning and evening prayers, praying the Angelus, partaking in Eucharist, reaffirming baptismal vows, and chanting out loud the Stations of the Cross — all fourteen of them — became the golden cord of God's grace made manifest that bound us together. The miracle was found in the pilgrimage itself. It was on this pilgrimage that my intellectualization of pilgrimage as a historical trivia item gave way. In its place came a new understanding of not only our common understanding of education in the church, but of the Christian life: Christians are on a pilgrimage, in which we are all pilgrims on the road, with no one and no other place to call home but God. Thankfully, the Roman Catholic Church continues to refer to the church as a pilgrim church. From that pilgrimage I came out with a ravenous appetite for more pilgrimages. I was particularly attracted to the small, exotic locations, like Chimayo, from Esquipulas, Guatemala, to St. Patrick's Purgatory in Ireland, places in which the "faithful" and the doubt-filled congregate out of an inner need, a divine calling, to remember whose we are. It is in these places that I continue to listen to and share pilgrimage narratives, celebrate the Eucharist, remember my baptism, and unload my list of griefs and gripes with the communion of saints. I have cried tears of penance on the rocky Penitential Beds of St. Patrick's Purgatory in Ireland, felt bewildered and alone in the cemetery of sister and brother monks in Lindisfarne — the Holy Isle — and experienced the deep wound of being a capitalistic oppressor amid the shanties in Esquipulas, Guatemala.

What all of these pilgrimage places share in common is the centrality of the cross of Christ. The cross was on the church where we would leave in the early morning, led us on the pilgrimage itself, or beckoned and welcomed the pilgrim home. The cross is not a dark smear upon human history, but a reminder of what, with God's help, we can all endure as God's good creation.

After my inaugural pilgrimage to Chimayo, the next time I follow a cross is with a class of five middle-class white men from Duke Divinity School, all in either their third year of studies or in post-graduate studies. They are students in a pilot course roughly titled, "Education of a Pilgrim." The goal of this Christian education course is to learn the practices of Christian pilgrimage as a way of educating Christians today. The strategies for reaching the goal included reading carefully and patiently a series of Christian pilgrimage narratives, from *Egeria's Travels* to the simple Russian tale *A Way of a Pilgrim,* and viewing some movies on video-tapes, like the Brazilian epic *Central Station.* We listened to the discourse between characters on pilgrimage, developed the plot of a pilgrimage itself, and discussed the rich themes of Christian pilgrimage. Students gained an intellectual grounding and shared understanding of the general characteristics of many Christian pilgrimages, in the past and the present, and its portent for the future. However, the unique strategy of teaching this course included taking the students on an actual pilgrimage so that they would have a physical, emotional, communal, and spiritual understanding of pilgrimage itself, hoping that they would understand themselves to be pilgrims at the end of the course. The students and I went on a two-day pilgrimage from Snow Camp to Durham, North Carolina, a distance of twenty-eight miles. The pilgrimage became the high point of the course as we all learned to expect the unexpected lessons of life, thanks to God's Spirit, who taught us much about ourselves and our community. It was on the pilgrimage that the readings, the movies, and the narratives of the students came together and the students' and professor's lives were changed forever.

The pilgrimage began in earnest on a Thursday at 9:00 a.m. Though I had tried to make plans for each part of the pilgrimage, I was excited yet nervous about the unexpected that is part and parcel of any pilgrimage. One of the educational characteristics of the pilgrimage is to, in part, let go of our expectations in order to see, hear, taste, touch, and be touched by the Holy Spirit in the richly textured fabric of creation.

We began by receiving the "Blessing of the Pilgrims on their Departure" from Mark Davidson, a Presbyterian pastor and friend:

> Brothers and sisters, as we set out, we should remind ourselves of the reasons for our resolve to go on this holy pilgrimage. The place we intend to visit is a monument to the devotion of the people of God. They have gone there in great numbers to be strengthened in the Christian way of life and to become more determined to devote themselves to the works of charity.

We left most of our luggage and sleeping bags in the sanctuary area of the church where we would sleep overnight, along with preparations for the evening meal. We took a student's minivan to a United Methodist Church in Snow Camp, a few miles northwest from Chapel Hill.

The first steps of this twenty-eight mile trek were rather ordinary. None of us remember anything outstanding. The sun was shining bright and unusually warm for this first week of December, even at 9:30 a.m. Like on the pilgrimage to Chimayo, we walked in single file along the roadside, alternating among the six of us the task of holding the six-foot cross of Christ made from branches that fell from a large oak tree during Hurricane Fran some years earlier. We chose the cross as a symbol for the public to know we were on a Christian pilgrimage. Every thirty minutes the group spent time either in silent contemplation, or talking among ourselves. Every hour we'd stop to sit and rest.

At twelve noon we stopped for lunch along the roadside. We ate sandwiches, some trail mix, sipped from the bottles of water we had brought along with us. The camaraderie among the pilgrims was genial, due in part to having been in class together for fifteen weeks. We still had no idea of what to expect during these two days.

The first encounter with the unexpected was when a deputy sheriff of the Orange County Sheriff Patrol stopped us. The deputy sheriff said there had been a call placed by one of the homeowners who lived along the roadway because they were suspicious of six young white men walking with a cross in this largely African American neighborhood. It was then that it dawned on me that a cross being carried so prominently in this part of the United States usually had to do with racist Ku Klux Klan activities. Carrying a cross in northern New Mexico was not as unusual or politically charged as carrying a cross in North Carolina, with a disturbing history of cross burnings on people's lawns late at night over the issues of race. Set in action was the power of carrying the cross, which also brought forth thought-provoking, heart-wrenching challenges for these two days.

With some trepidation I entered the sheriff's car, where the deputy sheriff asked about the purpose of the walk with the cross. He asked if I had a parade license or permit, and I told him no. Nervous, I also assured him that we weren't parading or protesting anything, but on a Christian pilgrimage as a class project on pilgrimage. He jotted down my name, the name of my school, my dean's name, and my home phone number. Smiling sheepishly, he said he did not remember a time when there was a group of Christian pilgrims walking this particular road. As I left the car he muttered, "God bless ya'."

With some relief of anxiety, the other pilgrims and I talked about this encounter, not sure if this were a church and state issue. Can the state tell us not to carry a cross? A connection between the readings and our lives and this pilgrimage was made as the students made reference to civil rights marches of the 1960s and the civil disobedience of Dorothy Day that we read about in class. We were genuinely surprised that we could have been seen as people having anything to do with the Klan. Yet this wouldn't be the only time that the racial tension of the southeastern part of this country and Christian pilgrimage would confront each other during this trek.

By the late afternoon we walked along Franklin Street in Chapel Hill, which is the main thoroughfare for the University of North Carolina–Chapel Hill. It is not a street unaccustomed to seeing protesters for one cause or other, displays of great exuberance when a university's sports team wins, or other cultural public fads. Some university students, faculty, and staff, townspeople and tourists, adults and children pointed at us as we walked silently along on the sidewalk with our six-foot cross. Now and then someone would wave at us; another person stopped and genuflected in front of the cross as we walked by; yet others would give us the "peace" sign or reach out to shake our hands warmly.

In the city block, the unexpected confronted us again: three men, all African American, older, each holding a small white box in one hand, on which was written the message that they were homeless and hungry, and that they needed money for the coming evening. "Have any spare change, mister?" said one of the beggars to the pilgrim holding the cross in the front of the line. The student holding the cross stopped in his tracks, and we stopped with him. "What do we do?" asked the befuddled student to the rest of us in the group. A chorus of "I don't knows," lasted a long minute while the people begging waited patiently, smiling at us, watching silently as we tried to figure out what we were going to do. Then the student holding the cross looked at the cross itself, and it dawned on him that he should do what Jesus would do in this situation: engage the men in conversation, listen to what they wanted, and probably give some money to them as well. Each one of us dug into our pockets, put some money in each person's box, and engaged in conversation.

The importance of this unexpected lesson was lost on no one. I was surprised, if not a little saddened, that it took such a long time for these students — all of whom were in their last years of seminary studies — to figure out what should be done in this situation. While I wanted to tell them what to do, I was held back by the thought, "Let them figure this one out on their own." It was a "teaching moment" in which the unplanned and unpredictable provided an unknown wealth of educational opportunities into the concrete, tangible, fleshy ways of Christ's body.

My sadness was lightened with joy at the unanimity of the generous response as we all placed money into their boxes. We each said "Have a good day" or something rather unremarkable as we left, unable to figure out what to say as a response to the magnanimous lesson given to us this day. The Presbyterian church where we were staying overnight was only two miles from this event, giving us plenty of time to reflect upon and discuss being stopped by the deputy sheriff and meeting those who are hungry and homeless "pilgrims."

One theological virtue learned along this pilgrimage was that these men were — for us — Christ, as we learned to perform the gestures of Scripture of Matthew 25:36, 40: "I was hungry and you gave me food.... Whatever you do to the least of these in my family you do to me." This was an incredible, unplanned lesson to learn from as we actively exegeted the Gospel of Matthew contextually and ecclesiologically. I was overjoyed as we were left struggling with the passage of Scripture with our very lives as we faced those who were hungry and homeless and we responded to the request by giving money to those who were begging. We did so against the claims of some in society that this money might not be spent for food or housing. Our gestures were tied to the Gospel according to Matthew in the very context of Franklin Street. We were performing the gestures of Christ, narrated by Scripture.

Moreover, we grappled with the text not as individuals but as a community of pilgrims who had spent all semester reading various pilgrimage narratives and sharing aspects of our personal lives openly with one another. We gave the money as a group and discussed what we encountered in giving money as a group.

Much of the discussion continued that evening while we were preparing, eating, and cleaning up after dinner, and over a beer or two. With overly zealous, pietistic tones, we focused on "church versus state" in the deputy sheriff's inquiry. We wondered aloud what the men were doing with the money we gave them that day. We discussed the power the teacher exercised in letting them learn from the experience itself. We also discussed the power of the cross of Christ in this southeastern Baptist and overtly racist culture versus the southwestern Catholic and differently racist culture of New Mexico. We reflected upon the power inherent in being white men walking with a cross in this time and place, and how politically charged is the cross of Christ, with various interpretations. As we pulled sleeping bags and pads together in the middle of the church's sanctuary, one of the students asked if we could spend the rest of the evening sharing our own *Canterbury Tales* with one another. Chaucer's "dare" to tell a good story about our lives while on the pilgrimage was the script for the evening: Scripture, old pilgrimage narratives, and our lives met each other in that moment. One by one we shared some of the events that revealed the lessons we had learned from our various lives. Each narrative went on for fifteen minutes, after which group members responded with questions. Each story was particular to the person; the only ground rule was that it be truthful and be about one's own life. Even in the sharing of our lives, each man became more vulnerable as we each shared intimate stories with others. We were continually being shaped into being more like a Christian community of pilgrims. All I remember from that evening was the sound of hearty laughter interjected between long periods of solemn silence amid stories of great sadness in the way some men's lives had been defiled and violated.

The next morning after wrapping up sleeping bags and pads, eating breakfast, and cleaning up, we then started before 7:30 a.m, on the trek along a major highway to Durham. We were to be met at twelve noon for lunch with Father David of Immaculate Conception Catholic Church in

Durham, our destination for our trek. We had walked six-teen miles the first day, leaving twelve miles this day. During the morning traffic rush there were many stares and people pointing fingers at us. The weather was December-warm again with no hints of rain.

We turned off the major highway onto a secondary road. There we were stopped by two young African American men in an old white Buick Le Sabre sedan. The passenger in the car rolled down his window and yelled: "What are you doing with the cross?" Unsure of the purpose of the passengers in the car, I told the driver it was a class project, and he wanted to know which class for what school. Satisfied with my answer, "Duke Divinity School, a Christian education class!" the driver made a U-turn in the road and drove away quickly. Racism came to the fore again as we carried the cross in this Klan-shrouded terrain. Six white guys with a tall cross walking through this part of the country, where African Americans have been lynched by some misguided racist religious zealots, were not a comforting presence.

We continued to walk on the crumbling roadway to Durham with the same schedule that we practiced the day before: alternating times of quiet with times of talking, along with a break to sit and eat once an hour. When we reached the sixth mile, one of the students said that a foot and knee pain that he experienced the day before was getting worse. Tears welled up in his eyes, and pain was etched across his brow. A mile later, this student was unable to walk. The progress of the pilgrimage was slowing down. A few more yards and we ground to a halt and talked about what we were going to do. Quoting the theme from the movie *White Squall*, we struggled with the reality of the statement: "Where we go one, we go all." Here we were, a gathering of pilgrims, and we had to figure out whether we were all going to make it, stop the pilgrimage here, or think of a third option, which we did: one person would get his car at the end of the pilgrimage, go pick up the student who was no longer able to walk, while the rest of us moved on to the Catholic church.

With grateful hearts, tired bodies, and a dissertation-worth of ideas on pilgrimage as education, we arrived at the Catholic church, and the hospitality of Father David, around twelve noon, right on schedule. Father David pulled together enough food for the gathering from the church's parish house kitchen, and we were all fed well. The ailing student and driver joined us. Around the table we shared with Father David many stories of the experiences which we had had on this pilgrimage, amazed at all that we had experienced, knowing that the full impact of the experienced wouldn't be felt right away, but many days, months, and years later. Even in this small exercise we were obviously not the same group of people who had left a day earlier: we were pilgrims. Something had happened: we were more of a community than we had been all semester, having shared together in a set of stories in these two days in ways that could never be repeated.

Father David then led us all to the sanctuary of the church where he began this time of closure with the "Blessing of Pilgrims after Their Return":

> Our pilgrimage has been a privileged period of grace given us by God. We who have come in trust to this holy place are moved with a new resolve to be renewed in heart. The sanctuaries that we have visited are a sign of the house not built with hands, namely, the body of Christ, in which we are the living stones built upon Christ, the cornerstone.

Our hunger and thirst satiated, the pilgrims sat in a circle in a small space in the front of the sanctuary. We each reflected upon the ways our lives were impacted in less than forty-eight hours: bearing witness to Christ, we experienced the racism of the South; we met poverty face-to-face; we reflected anew upon the course's readings as we added our own stories to *Canterbury Tales;* and we were supportive of one another when some people were most weak and vulnerable, emotionally as well as physically. We became a gathering of pilgrims.

We came out quietly from the sanctuary, thanking Father David for his gracious hospitality, and some went back to the car to go back to Chapel Hill to get our luggage. One pilgrim went back to his house to soak his aching feet and knees in hot water; others went home to spouses or loved ones; all of us went back to catch up on sleep. I took the cross back to my office.

The pilgrimage was over for that day. But the lessons of God's grace in a beautiful North Carolina meadow, of walking with a cross through a tortured land of racism, of learning to be generous with the Christ before us, and to discover the presence of Christian community among ourselves as we cared for our fallen companion will last forever.

Chapter Four

Seeking the Christ

The Christ you seek you will not find, unless you bring him with you.
— Anonymous

Our pilgrimage to Esquipulas, Guatemala, began innocently enough with a conversation with Sister Stefanie, O.S.B., at St. John's Abbey and University's Alcuin Library. It was only later I would laugh at God's providential hand once again shoving me to a place of surprising growth. Stefanie was referred to me after I shared with others at the university that I was studying the broad and general topic of "pilgrimage." At the time, my interest in pilgrimage was primarily an intellectual bauble. I wasn't in search of finding something that would be "life-changing," throwing me into a whole new galaxy of ideas. Without willful choice, the seed of pilgrimage was sown already, and pilgrimage's roots were taking hold in my convoluted life.

When I asked Stefanie about pilgrimage in her rather plain library office, her eyes lit up and the room started to glow as she grew more animated, telling me of the special place of Esquipulas, Guatemala. For hundreds of years prior to the Spanish "discovery" — or conquest — of the area, the Mayan people in the vicinity, who spoke Chorti, made pilgrimage to this place. When the Spaniards came into the area, Chief Esquipulas offered no resistance, so as to avoid the slaughtering of the people. The town was then called

Santiago de Esquipulas in honor of the Chief. And with the Spanish settlers, the place was still identified and strengthened as a site for pilgrimage. For the last hundred years, Christian pilgrims from all over central America — Chiapas, Guatemala, Belize, Panama, Costa Rica, Honduras, El Salvador — and other places throughout the world have come to this place, this site, and have been welcomed as they come to venerate, adore, and give thanks to the Black Christ — the crucifix of Nuestro Señor de Esquipulas — for the miracles performed in their ordinary lives. More powerfully, the pilgrimage is a sign of the gift of inspired faith that provokes them — and us — to pay homage with our very lives in venerating El Cristo Negro.

As an Anglo, middle-class American Protestant — a Presbyterian at that — I wasn't sure either who El Cristo Negro was or where in the world Esquipulas was, let alone know how to speak Spanish, with or without a Guatemalan accent. I listened politely as her soft voice grew increasingly strong and passionate, describing to me small clay cakes, made at a nearby clay pit, with certain healing powers; the image of *El Christo Negro*, named for the Christ figure sculpted from dark wood four hundred years ago, with Mary his mother, Mary Magdalene, and St. John on a holy death watch from the unsafe sidelines; the immensely grandiose but worn-down-by-age Spanish ornateness of the colonial baroque basilica and some of the faithful and very human Benedictine monks who embody Benedictine hospitality in serving the pilgrims and Christ there; the pilgrims who shuffle on their knees to venerate Christ; and Stefanie's many friends, who included older men and women and their children from the growing neighborhood sprawl of rich and poor living together. And she told me of the interior of the basilica with the burning candles and the repeated sound of prayers for salvation from oppression and poverty; prayers of gratitude out of love for the Christ and miraculous healing of their lives; pleas of mercy while begging for forgiveness for an affair gone awry.

To be sure that the seed is planted, a year later — during my sabbatical break — Stefanie gives me a postcard of El Cristo Negro. I am transfixed by the solitary, hauntingly gentle Christ hanging lifeless from the cross, his eyes closed, weary from this humiliating spectacle; a crown of thorns fitting snugly firmly thrust upon his head. His body is exhausted ... all life is drained away. Mary's head is bent down in sorrow, grieving for the loss of her dead son. Only the intricate gold halos on their heads shine in the empty darkness of death.

Stefanie asks if I am planning to go on pilgrimage in October. Without thinking about it, I simply say, "yes." The seed is planted deeply in my imagination; I yearn to see what awaits me in Esquipulas, and within less than a year, I was on my way to Guatemala. Esquipulas is a town on the southeastern border of Guatemala with Honduras: "Honduras is less than twenty-five kilometers" I am told by many in Esquipulas. Further south is the border of El Salvador, and to the northeast is Belize. Having left North Carolina at 6:50 a.m., meeting up with Stefanie in Houston, I feel more like lost Dorothy in the strange land of Oz without her Toto; I rub my eyes when we arrive at the 1960s-style Guatemalan airport in the center of Guatemala City at 1:00 p.m. It is older, dingy yellow in its current appearance — a noticeable change from the gleaming, sterile white modern airports of the States. The mosaics are losing tiles bit by bit; its wall of international clocks frozen in time showing different hours of the day in Tokyo, New York City, and London. "Bienvenidos" scream two large cheery, garishly painted billboards outside the terminal, and underneath are throngs of citizens.

The citizenry was magnificent in their beautiful, smooth brown skin. In a week's time, I came to see the slight differences between the indigenous Guatemalans — many from the mountains that ring Guatemala City, who have a smaller stature due to diet, almost almond-shaped eyes, a nose that is connected with the prominent forehead, high cheek bones, beautiful full lips, and straight jet-black hair — and those with a Spanish heritage, whose hair may be curly or straight, whose eyes are like any other person with a European heritage like mine, are of average height, yet are also brown of skin. As my friends remind me, this brown face is the face of the future of all the Americas: North, Central, and South.

On the plane, and now on the way out of the terminal, Stefanie and I are surrounded by Guatemalans as well as by a cadre of white, middle-class, fervent, God-fearing American fundamentalists. They are coming for a major evangelical conference in this Catholic country, sponsored by a "convert" to American evangelicalism — and capitalism — President Alfonso Portillo of Guatemala: "Let Jee-ssuss embrace your heart!" pled the young evangelical clutching his heart in front of me on the plane as if he had a heart attack, trying to woo an older Catholic man who kept on saying he lived three hours away from Guatemala City and couldn't come to the rally for "Jee-ssuss" at the main site of the rally, El Shaddai. A handful of happy yellow-vested Guatemalan tour guides are there to welcome the Americans amid the throng of poorer Guatemalans in front of me. Seeing I am an American they ask, "Are you needing a ride to the rally?" Before I can answer, Stefanie and I are saved from the evangelical horde by the only other white face I see amid a sea of brown faces: Brother Robert, who welcomes us with his lilting New Orleans accent, taking our luggage to a van that whisks us away to Esquipulas. By chance I notice a young gunman guarding the airport parking lot, keeping away the average citizen, with barbed wire in metal ringlets encircling the chain-link fenced parking lot. High fences, barbed wire, and gunmen: common tourist scenes in Guatemala.

We then leave for a five-hour road trip from Guatemala City to Esquipulas along a two-lane "highway," much of which is brand new and still being paved. As the light of the first day leaves us in this central time zone, we pass people walking on the street to and fro, women balancing — with seeming ease — large three-gallon striped clay or plastic water jars on their heads while walking hand-in-hand with their children on either side. A cluster of poor people sell crops from the nearby fields for next-to-nothing prices. In the tropical forest on the side of the road we occasionally see signs of a house — or shack — with its tile or tin roof and adobe walls made of painted or unpainted mud. Cinder-block construction is a luxury for many but necessary, as termites are always eating away at any wood structure, save for the harder woods. Blue Bird buses, used for public schools in the States, are packed tightly with people, some of them pilgrims, going to or from cities along the way. No longer yellow, the buses are painted bright, exotic colors, from teal to purple, and the roofs are piled high with bags and produce tied down with yards of rope; most of the produce is to be sold in the town and village streets along the way. We pass a herd of cattle lumbering slowly on the highway, unfazed as we zoom past in the white minivan, drawing closer to Esquipulas.

The last hour is spent on a zig-zag course up a daunting mountain pass road with a one-lane bridge still barely useable, and then descending steeply. Suddenly, as we take one more sharp hairpin turn, our eyes feast on the breathtaking beauty before us: the starry twinkling lights outlining Esquipulas in the valley below. A wrought iron gate automatically opens up for us as we enter the quiet, lush grounds of the Benedictine monastery. I fail to see the poor shanty across the street. Welcome to the paradoxical paradise of Esquipulas.

On Tuesday morning I walk out into the sunlit courtyard of the hacienda-style white stucco monastery with its red tile roof, second-floor balconies, and red brick walkways. I am struck by the ever-present lush vegetation and abundant garden greenery: roses and hibiscus, orange birds of paradise and day lilies. Near the monastery library there are mounds and row upon row of day lilies, a favorite project of the former abbot, Father Matthew, who was trying to cultivate a new flower: the Black Christ day lily. The most recent blossom is a deep-burnt orange, almost black. In the ponderous cultivation process, it takes years to breed such a hybrid blossom. But this is the land of "eternal spring," never too hot or too cold, with always the promise of some clouds and a dash of rain during the day with a pinch of hopeful sunshine nurturing the verdant forest of kaleidoscopic budding blossoms and "bodacious" blooms. In the middle of the courtyard is a worn, large stone cross, with a statue of Mary in one of the many alcoves, hidden among the enormous palm fronds and elephant grass edging.

Morning prayers are prayed every morning at 6:00 a.m. in the basilica, followed by Mass at 6:30 a.m., all in Spanish. I am late the first morning — and almost every morning — and quietly enter the choir section, rubbing the gritty sleep out of my eyes and scratching my bed-head hair going all kinds of ways. I sneak around the large brown organ and sit next to Stefanie, who has arranged for me all the books needed for praying the psalms in the morning. The morning psalms are chanted quickly, almost on one sustained note, and my early morning tongue bungles and slurs alien words together. I smile when we say "el Señor," one word I understand. As I look to my left I spy pilgrims already there, some seated in the few pews in the front of the basilica. There is an initial scattering of white candles burning in the large black tin trays near the altar rail. The trays would be filled to overflowing in a few minutes — a sea of fire — with some pilgrims melting the bottom of the candles and sticking them already lit on the flagstone floor: there is a two-tier layer of candles burning brightly before the Christ, sending wave upon wave of smoky thanks to the Lord of the heavens. By the late afternoon, people look like tightrope walkers as, with outstretched hands, they pick their way carefully between the burning candles, appearing from a distance as if they are walking amid a bonfire. Soon the basilica custodians dutifully begin their hourly ritual of scraping the paper ribbon and melted wax off the floor and gently putting still burning candles from the floor into a vacant spot on the black trays. By the late afternoon and evening I smelled burned candle wicks and saw the basilica full of gray candle smoke, leaving a fog inside which was barely cut through by the streaking shafts of sunlight, with a dull gray residue left on the freshly painted white walls and columns.

Stefanie and I sit in the mahogany-wood choir stall, along with a few of the monks in their black hooded habits and some of the young seminarians. Brother Robert expertly plays the Anderson organ. There are a few other Anglos among the monks, as the monastery was founded in 1959 with Benedictine brothers from St. Joseph Abbey outside of New Orleans who came to Esquipulas after the bishop of

Guatemala made three invitations. Father Matthew was the first abbot, followed by the current Abbot Gregory, who is literally a "survivor" of cancer — as much as one can survive cancer.

The white-walled basilica was built in the 1700s for the primary purpose of housing the Black Christ. Originally located in the smaller parish church up the road, Calle Real, El Cristo Negro was brought to this home with much celebrative fanfare, or so the records show. The Spanish baroque design of the basilica includes four huge towers that stand guard at each corner of the building; large-as-life statues of St. Anthony and other saints of the church are standing sentinel, set into small portals around the building, almost reverent in their posture as they silently gaze upon the mass of pilgrims who come here daily. A grand staircase leads from the green park in front of the basilica, to the tall, worn wooden doors open to the pilgrims who come, with the words *Año Santo–Jubileo 2000* and colorful posters for the Jubilee Year on the inside of the door. On special days during the Jubilee Year the doors are ringed with green palm fronds.

Through these doors the faith-filled pilgrims come steadily, from the lowliest and simplest of people to the famous, like the late Salvadoran Archbishop Oscar Romero, Pope John Paul II, and Mother Teresa and other Missionaries of Charity. The monks tell me that Romero came here for a retreat a month before he was shot by military forces in El Salvador; the Sisters of Mercy continue to come. In the next few days I would watch and meet pilgrims whose quiet or exuberant grace-filled devotion to the Christ revealed a passionate love and perseverance of faith. Some come to give thanks to Christ for a healing. Others are searching for hope against the backdrop of hopeless poverty and life-stripping, death-gripping oppression. Yet even amid the poverty — the poorest of the poor — I witness a gentle beauty, a dignity among these very same people. And in their homes, among their families, there is a warmth, a love which arises surprisingly from a life that is harsh by any standards in the States. Some are caught in an endless, daily fight to survive; others come with much education and riches beyond measure. On one afternoon I watch as a young fifteen-year-old woman enters into the basilica for her *quinceaños* celebration, pretty in a pink dress, her black hair full of flowers. Yet in the next few minutes six men carry in a simple wooden coffin, the remains of a town leader of Esquipulas. An infant baptism is celebrated an hour later. What unites them all is the common need to give thanks to the Christ in this place, this holy ground.

On the first days in Esquipulas my pilgrimage included a walk up the tall hill on the edge of town: the walk up El Calvario is marked by fourteen Stations of the Cross. The way to the hill is through one of the main thoroughfares of town, passing the many little shops that sell Orange Crush and Pepsi, *tiendas,* each shop painted white and Pepsi blue. Many of the larger and more expensive homes are closer to the city of thirteen thousand people, with the smaller, poorer abodes further up the hill and away from the city center. A small Ford Escort, a Toyota truck, and a fast-moving motor scooter zip by us; marimba music is heard from a house; a young man wears his Nike shirt and hat proudly as he walks down the street. The sidewalk ends; we walk the muddy road that soon becomes a bumpy cobblestone trail. Higher on the hill the homes have no barbed wire or beautiful wrought iron fences and gates, for there is little in these homes that anyone would steal. On my right and left are low-lying homes with their tin roofs, a rough window without glass but perhaps wooden shutters; a simple wooden door without a lock; a kitchen that includes a pot and an open-air fireplace; no running water or sewer system. Yet some have electricity for the television set, with a cord running out from the house to the nearest electric wire high on a wooden pole on the street. A scrawny chicken runs underfoot... perhaps tonight's dinner for a family. A thin, starving dog, with swollen teats, obviously ill, walks by in a lethargic state. Children, wearing no shoes and laced with dirt, run happily after a shell of a ball, laughing with great abandon in this simple game. A small house has row upon row of white ceramic figures — a small donkey equal in size to the Christ child — used for nativity scenes. The homes are the center for the cottage industry of making all kinds of candles, candies, figurines, and hats reminding people of their pilgrimage to Esquipulas and the blessings of El Cristo Negro.

At the top of the hill is a small chapel, now closed and locked, with dry flowers and partly burnt candles; a mom-and-pop Pepsi booth is there for thirsty pilgrims. A weathered stone-gray cross sits atop the chapel, and a rusted bell, vines entwined around it, stands guard on a rickety stand. We stroll the small plaza outside of the chapel, looking in all directions, taking in the beauty of Esquipulas: a soccer field; larger homes on the fringes; wisps of cloud seeming to come out of the surrounding mountainside, as if the mountains' forests were on fire, sending aloft a smoky fog. And seated in the middle of it all is the precious white jewel of the basilica, shining in the distance, set upon the green velvet cushiony trees surrounding it.

We walk back to the basilica along the city streets. We can buy anything on the streets, from compact disk stereos to bananas and red meat. Surrounding the park-like grounds of the basilica, with its carefully manicured green lawns and fountains, there are seemingly hundreds of small shops that sell remembrances for the pilgrims. For example, there are small straw hats with the colorful corona around them. The corona looks like a skinny raccoon's tail brightly painted with stripes of yellow, red, green, and blue, which can adorn hats as well as car antennas or luggage racks, proof positive that you were a pilgrim to Esquipulas. There are candles of all shapes and sizes, some in glass votive containers, others with colorful streamers around them which will soon adorn the floor and trays of the basilica. There are the small clay cakes, made with fine white kaolin mined from nearby caves. They are called *pan del Señor* (bread of the Lord). These tablets were once taken by those who were pregnant or in need of medical attention, with the element of faith always the important part of the ingestion. Other vendors sell straw baskets filled with candies and cakes wrapped tightly in yellow cellophane. All of these are sold around the basilica in brightly decorated booths, some with large beach umbrellas protecting them from the noonday sun.

One unforgettable image is the blessing of these remembrances by the black-hooded monks: outside, on one side of the basilica, people line up in three or four long rows near poles saying *Bendición,* placing their treasures in front of them on the ground. The monks then come with red and yellow plastic buckets of blessed water and bless the people and their remembrances, the pilgrims' heads bent in reverence. Now blessed, people return home to family members who could not come on pilgrimage, bringing with them a blessed reminder of the goodness of Christ.

The only thing for sale on the grounds of the basilica park are Polaroid snapshots taken by photographers, showing that one has come to venerate El Cristo Negro. By special permission, some few people with disabilities are allowed to ask for donations in the park. In a magical twist of "foolishness to the Greeks," the men I meet with disabilities are the first and the last persons pilgrims meet when they arrive or depart from the basilica. In the reality of God's kingdom, these are Christ in our world, lodged in the heart, body, and mind of these otherwise disabled people. It is Jesus who is already there to welcome and to say *adios* to the mass of pilgrims.

This is the destination for many pilgrims for hundreds of years. There is a crass commercialism of pilgrimage here — like the Hotel El Peregrino with "TV, Cable, and Hot Water" next door to the basilica — alongside the humblest of pilgrims who saved all year to come back to Esquipulas to give thanks to the Christ for a miracle or a blessing in their lives, thus keeping a promise to come back once a year. I watch, listen, touch, smell, and walk with this living procession through time in a place in which the pilgrims' procession *is* the record of knowledge of the disciplined life of the pilgrim, and the holiness of El Cristo Negro survives and is communicated from one generation to the next. Such knowledge isn't in books, essays, travel videos, computer disks, websites, or still photographs. The knowledge of the life of one of Christ's pilgrims is in the people, in the landscape; it is in the very act of walking across a terrain of mountains and hills, bearing physical witness to the Stations of the Cross and coming on one's knees before El Cristo Negro in a basilica where the needs and prayers, joys and concerns of people reverberate throughout God's time and the omnipotent reaches of God's reign of love. How do I know this for certain? I watch and listen studiously to the pilgrims. Whether sitting in the choir stalls of the basilica, walking in the park in front of the basilica, running along the streets of the city, stopping by a booth to buy something for home as a remembrance, or interviewing the pilgrims themselves, I am in awe of the gestures of faith performed either effortlessly or with great grace by these pilgrims.

One morning during Mass I hear a shuffling of something against the hard geometrically designed flagstone floor of the basilica. As I watch, in a single row, in typical dress woven by the indigenous people in the mountains and hills of Guatemala, three women shuffle forward on their knees. They have been shuffling from the front door of the basilica all the way to the altar, past confessionals and statues. Each is wearing a shawl over her head, with the last woman carrying a baby on her back in a red woven shawl. Their faces are the beautiful faces of native or indigenous people, not of Spanish descent. They murmur the rosary on the way to the altar rail, carrying candles forward to give thanks to the Christ. Then, without turning around — for one never turns one's back on El Cristo Negro — they shuffle backward on their knees in a single file out of the basilica.

Stefanie and I were given the "monk's tour" of the basilica on the evening we arrived, walking around with Brother Robert as he told us the story of the various life-size statues of saints, large marble altars, simple confessionals, and small chapels on the interior periphery of the basilica. We walked up to the Plexiglas paneling around the shrine which is meant to protect El Cristo Negro from the wear and tear of touching, age, and candle smoke. It is set behind the altar with all its ornate silver and its beautiful, colorful, intricately woven Guatemalan cloths, surrounded by large and colorful silk flowers — real flowers are also left by pilgrims and fill in the nearby space. I pick a fresh blossom of nard, whose perfume lasts all week long in my monastic room.

In this small sanctum, the solitary black sculpture of Christ stands out among the gleaming white faces of those witnessing his death. This statue of the Christ was carved by a Portuguese artisan, Quirio Catano, in Antigua, Guatemala. This five-foot figure is made of balsam and orange wood, giving it a dark hue. Moreover, years of candles and incense have turned the image to a smoky black. The darkness of the wood made it easier for the native Chorti people of Esquipulas to accept the Christ of dark complexion like themselves. This Christ figure is on a silver cross, which is itself richly decorated with sculptured vines and painted golden leaves. In 1595 the finished figure was brought to the town of Esquipulas and housed in a little chapel which was built upon the site of a native shrine close to several health-giving springs. The image of Christ was soon known for the miraculous healings that followed it on its way from Guatemala City to Esquipulas. The archbishop of Guatemala, Pedro Pardo de Figuerora, was cured of a contagious disease during his visit to the shrine in 1737, and out of gratitude he ordered the construction of the present sanctuary, which was completed in 1758, with the archbishop's body buried in the basilica.

For a week I watched the faithful stream close to El Cristo Negro. The way to come close was by a serpentine back entrance to the basilica. Along a winding path, I passed a life-size statue of the Christ figure on hands and knees, half naked, with his back flayed open and bleeding from the whips that cut his skin, his face caught in utter pain, but no sound coming forth. On the walls are large frames with tiny metal and plastic plaques (*ex votos*), as well as figures of arms and legs which were left with messages of gratitude to Christ for a miracle in one's life, like a healing of a broken leg, arm, or another part of the body.

When you are in the vicinity of the Black Christ, you approach from behind the Christ. Then, to honor the Christ, it is customary to leave this moving scene by walking backward, never turning one's back on the Christ.

A twist that endeared the veneration of this Christ to my Protestant sensibilities of mind and heart: pilgrims came to visit the Christ not seeking a miracle right then and there. Rather, they came to this place to thank Christ for the miracles either already performed in their lives, or to take this time to pray for a special need, yet always in a spirit of thankfulness for life itself, no matter how rich or poor, healthy or ill one is. Simple gestures of thankfulness and deep gratitude are the primary impulse for the many coming on pilgrimage to Esquipulas.

Perhaps the statement that most accurately captures what is the right gesture before this Christ is what I heard often in Esquipulas: "The Christ you seek you will not find unless you bring him with you." Many people come here not in search of Christ, faith, grace, love, or hope. Rather, they come here bringing Christ within them. It is the Christ within them who makes this place holy ground. It is more than an inner gut feeling or theological tourist treat. They are created in the image of God, and it is Christ within them who gives the pilgrims the spontaneous impetus, the burning desire, the unquenchable need, to venerate El Cristo Negro.

I see a group of pilgrims from Belize. You can tell they are from Belize — probably Livingston — I am advised, because they are of African descent. From afar, I am struck by the largeness of the women and the slender men. The women wear bright clothes of yellows and whites and pinks, perhaps a plaid; each woman also wears a bandana or hat as a covering over her head. Some women are easily balancing straw baskets or black luggage on the top of their heads, while others carry large cloth handbags full of remembrances: candies and cookies, crosses and small figurines of El Cristo Negro. They stand in roughly two lines at the bottom of the grand stairs leading up to the basilica, praying out loud and singing songs of praise. An older, larger woman, gripped by extreme passion, throws herself prostrate onto the pavement, beating her fists against the hard stone. The voices of the people around her continue to swell in volume in their chanting and praying and singing in Creole around this woman who is obviously gripped by a need to make fervent, dramatic appeals to the Almighty God who alone can save her from her agony and answer her urgent prayers. No one tries to pick her up or stop her from praying. Rather, they all surround her and support her appeal to the One alone who can meet her deepest, unspeakable needs.

There is the illogical necessity of the divine extravagance being played out and performed among the pilgrims who gather here at Esquipulas basilica before El Cristo Negro. An extravagance or madness to leave one's home far away, to take one's immediate and extended family on a trip some distance away, and leave a job that already pays too little for maintaining one's day-to-day, meal-by-meal existence, all for the sake of visiting El Señor de Esquipulas.

Many families can literally *not* afford this trip financially. The divine necessity driving pilgrims from within is the belief bred within them, generation after generation, that all of life is a gift of God's giving, and that any healing of body, mind, and spirit comes from God alone who, in the person of Jesus Christ and the tangible presence of the Holy Spirit, sides with and advocates on behalf of the oppressed poor, the homeless, the widow, the orphan, and the sick. Out of an almost unconscious holy habit, the pilgrims come to give thanks to Christ, venerating the Christ for an hour or even longer, burning candles, worshiping God during the celebration of the Eucharist. Such worship becomes or renews the center of one's very being: here, we are not individual pilgrims, wandering by our lonesome selves; here, we are members, one of another, of a community of other pilgrims who gather with us in this place, with Christ *in* them. We become part of the ever-growing cloud of witnessing saints who are ever before us along the pilgrim way to the kingdom of God. It is the people of God who make this place, this time, holy, and not the things in and of themselves. It is the people who bring the Christ already in them to Esquipulas, whose light burns brighter and warmer within and among them as they — and we — gather and perform the gesture and receive the promise that, wherever two or three are gathered in Jesus' name, the one also among us is the Christ.

The potency of this necessary extravagance came to the fore while I was at early morning Eucharist on Sunday morning. It was in the words of the priest delivering the homily and uttering the words of institution; it was in the beautiful singing of the choirs of people around me, and Brother Robert's extraordinary ability to pull out gorgeous music, key-by-key, from the aged organ. Before me is a life-size statue of Mary standing in a maroon robe. There is the swirling mist of smoke from the black trays already filled with candles of all kinds of sizes, the floor below sprinkled liberally with candles as well as with the candles' glow. Throngs of people are lined up row upon row along the railing that barely keeps them away from the altar. It is in the moment that the priest is breaking the bread, "the body of Christ," pouring the cup of salvation that I am caught up in a swirling, dizzying, movement of the Spirit that has been moving underneath the surface of this reality for some time. My dull attention catches on to what is arising and enveloping me in the holy choreographed chaotic gyrations: a handsome young man, Latino and macho, with a beautiful dark complexion and chiseled face, his white shirt unbuttoned slightly, has dropped the machismo of his culture and is crying on his knees, his left hand holding two white candles with ribbons around them, freshly lit as they are still long tapers, while his right hand is in a fist, as he shakes it toward El Cristo Negro: he is speaking directly to the Christ through sobs. "Holy, holy, holy Lord, God of power and might" the congregation responded in unison and firmly in Spanish. "And on the night that he was betrayed," says the priest. One of the pilgrims from Belize, a large older woman, is in tears as she stands up against the shrine. On her tiptoes she is straining to push up a small boy's T-shirt, perhaps for a grandson or nephew, wanting to be sure that the closed eyes of the Black Christ make contact and bless the shirt and thus the wearer. More shirts come out of the bag at her side. She pushes them up, one by one, crying and praying and singing at the same time. "Amen," intones the priest, and moves to serve the people close to the railing.

With the help of Miguel and Oscar Capriel, two "natives" of Esquipulas, we listen and receive in gratefulness, laughing and crying in empathy, the stories of a scattered group of pilgrims: one group of women says they come yearly to pray, asking God to grant their hopes. Another extended family with twelve adults and twelve children — multiple generations — come every year en masse, asking for the health of those members in the family who are sick and unable to come. Some come by the Blue Bird bus; others come by private cars, while Miguel tells me he saw a group riding toward town on horses. One family of four comes once a year because the mother started coming when she was a young girl with her family: "We come because we have faith God is everywhere, though there is something special about coming to Esquipulas ... God blesses you everywhere and every day." One family of three came with a long written list of things to thank God for, as well as another list asking God to "bless our business, bless our crops and harvest, and give long life to our sons."

Another extended family gathering comes out of the basilica. The matriarch of the family tells us that when she passes the Christ she feels like she is going to cry: "People begin to cry when they move from the back of the Christ to the front of the Christ because they are so thankful," she tells us.

Another young man I watch from afar: he is on his knees in the large doorway, his arms stretched out and raised to the heavens, crying to God. He comes over to tell us that he is from Honduras, which is where his family is from, and that "God has a warm heart for Honduras." Over and over again, pilgrims tell me they come here to thank God, to thank Christ in Esquipulas for all the good things in life, like good health, a new car, a new baby in the family, or because of the miracle they've received from the Christ, but can't tell us what "because that's private." One woman is hesitant to tell me anything because she isn't sure if I am a believer in the Black Christ or one of those "Seventh-Day Adventists," who just moved into town. Not too far away from the basilica is a Mormon church. Convinced of my sincerity, she tells us that she has come "because of the promises of God in Christ, who shows us love because there are always miracles."

A group of three men tell us that they came here because of their curiosity over the legend of El Señor de Esquipulas. I suppress a laugh as one of the men wears a black T-shirt with the initials "KKK" on it, a Confederate flag coloring each letter, and yet he is oblivious to its meaning. A pair of giddy young women, with all kinds of pilgrimage remembrances, arrive together in town to celebrate the youngest one's birthday.

One older couple have come from El Salvador for two years in a row. They come because they promised the Christ to come each year, and they have faith in the Christ to cure them of their illness: the husband to be cured of his back pain, and the wife to be cured of leg pains. They come because when they go home their health is usually restored after venerating, giving thanks to the Christ.

I am the pilgrim from North Carolina. I buy my two white candles with Mylar strips around them, melt the rough end and light the wick, planting the candle in the crowded tray, and sit next to a brother, a sister, in Christ's body and pray a litany of thanks: Thanks for this eye-opening, heart-expanding pilgrimage; for Benedictine hospitality; for children's laughter, parents' adulation, and friends' unswerving support for crazy dreams; for book projects accepted and others on hold; for significant relationships — for love; for dogs and cats who bring mirth into homes; for students at Duke Divinity School who bring both joy and frustration. Stefanie buys me a small silver medallion of the Black Christ tableau to accompany my St. Benedict's medal that I wear around my neck. I am marked as a pilgrim of El Señor de Esquipulas.

Chapter Five

COMPANIONS ALONG THE WAY

It was a cold December day, especially by North Carolina standards: below thirty-two degrees, drizzling rain, a cold, wet blanket of ice on the landscape. There was just enough of a chill to cut through all kinds of fabric to raw skin. A week earlier, we were under a snowstorm watch, with predictions of ten to twelve inches of the white stuff. Getting out of a warm bed, the dog lying beside us, was hard enough. But opening the door of the house that morning to leave for a marathon was either courage . . . or lunacy. Who wants to run up and down hills for 26.2 miles on a cloudy, rainy, bone-chilling gray December morning?

Over one thousand people greeted one another on that cold morning on what has become a modern day "pilgrimage": a marathon. At 7:00 in the morning the Raleigh Convention Center was surrounded by bus after bus. The buses were there to take runners on relay teams to their designated drop-off spots. A lone wheelchair marathoner was hunched over in his slick aluminum chariot. Given a fifteen-second advantage, he wheeled into place and took off with a blow of a whistle while we waited for the gun, counting backward, "3, 2, 1," and *bang* went the gun, and shuffle went the runners!

The array of dress was unlike any other pilgrimage I had been on: there was a man dressed like Spiderman in an orange tank-top. Others had on colorful long sleeve shirts, stocking or baseball caps or both on their heads. There was Vaseline on cheeks, lips, hands. Some wore gloves; others wore Lycra stockings on hands, arms, legs, and feet. Shoes were a bright array or rainbow of color, with all kinds of treads. And the small cheering crowd on the corner was dressed for the cold morning, rooting for the runners with a muffled roar because of the mittened hands and scarves over mouths.

When we heard the countdown along with "On your mark, runners..." or something like that, we did not move much. It was all rather anti-climatic as no one was moving at first. We just stood there in the back of the pack, talking, laughing, and looking silly. But like a slow roll of the wave on the beach, my bunch in the back of the pack began making a slight shuffling move, moving quicker by the second, until we broke into a comfortable stride.

The first two miles went effortlessly. I did not feel my feet hit the pavement, and I could not believe how quickly the miles went by me. No pilgrimage was like *this* one, with the slow, somber pace. This was exciting.

Like a pilgrimage, though, the beginning of a marathon or any walk is not all wrapped up in the first step or the initial mile. I ran a marathon when I was in my late twenties, and I had not thought about ever doing one again, until I had gone on a pilgrimage, and thought: "These two are more alike than unalike, but how? And why do it now?

On the one hand, I ran the marathon for all the vain and glorious reasons that any one in their forties runs: I am a white American male, father of two, in fairly good physical condition, and I had to prove I could do it, just like I had to prove I could walk over one hundred miles on a pilgrimage!

But a marathon takes a different kind of training: it meant sticking to a running schedule, being disciplined to run longer and faster, eat a certain diet, and consume enough water to please a fish in a fish bowl.

On the other hand, I ran the marathon for the same reason I go on pilgrimage: for a new experience in life that seems to mirror the hurly-burly, jumble, and spill of my so-called life. Running the marathon was another way for me to remember that there are long stretches in life in which I have to keep my eye on the prize before me, setting goals and attaining them, amid all the book projects, teaching duties, pastoral duties, family activities, and church programs that leave me anxious and breathless and feeling stress. Running, like going on pilgrimage, helps me put it all into perspective. Running and walking a pilgrimage provide the space, the time, the companionship, the schedule, the rigor, the feeling of "being accomplished" at something when everything else seems beyond my control.

It was running *this* marathon, however, while writing this book on pilgrimage that I came to appreciate anew how these modern civic marathons — no longer the province of Olympic Grecian glories — are a modern pilgrimage of sorts. Marathons are not restricted to the svelte, taut, muscular divas and heroes of the track and field world. We modern marathoners are like Bunyan's hapless "Christian," leaving a certain place, perhaps from a tired image of self or burnt-out jobs and families, to find our "Celestial City" at the end of the day as we cross the "wicket Gate" of a finish line, with a "heavenly host," a great gathering of family and friends to meet us at the destination's end.

Or like Chaucer's motley crew of pilgrims to Canterbury, we enter conversations with unexpected acquaintances — and perhaps new friends — that God sends along the way and the journey becomes the focus of the pilgrimage itself.

Dressed in purple tights, small knit hats, fancy red sweat-shirts, and tight tank tops were people who were fat and thin, tall and short, with or without that ageing "spare tire" or "love handle" waistline. We are today's Chaucerian characters of knights, serfs, monks, prioress, and the wife of Bath is running slightly ahead of me. The persons who cross that finish line are not the same person who left the starting line, because they have, with their own body, mind, and spirit and the support of friends on the sidelines, accomplished the goal of taking one step at a time until they cross the finish line, our glorious destination. At that time, we are all changed, like pilgrims are in their reaching their journey's end: we change from amateur to veteran marathoner!

Mile One: This first mile is painless. I feel free, liberated. The breeze is more like a windy reminder that we are closer to winter than we are to summer, especially when running up a hill or between buildings in downtown Raleigh. It is great to have the wind at my back, pushing me up the rolling hills, but damning me when it becomes a bullish head wind. My hands become red, raw, and numb; my cheeks grow to reddish rouge healthiness, though my head begins to sweat underneath my favorite orange baseball cap: it is the same cap I have always worn on pilgrimage!

Running the marathon I am aware of my body. I am no longer a man in a car, man at writing desk, man divorced from the land or the road or the building, man divorced from his feelings of his own body. I am my body. I feel my skin stretch, my large bones and hamstring muscles, nerve endings tingling and twisting joints, new aches and old pains revisited. I am filleted to the marrow of my being: I am more aware of my body's movement and place within the physical world than at any other time or circumstance.

I note the changes along the way as my body keeps moving forward, inch by inch, mile by mile, toward the finish line. I feel the sole of my feet burning at one point, the center of my sole shifting slightly; I run to the top ridge of a hill and the pain dissipates. I feel the top of my left foot; a bone is being rubbed where my shoelaces come together. But as I shift my left foot to the outside of the shoe, the pain is gone!

Mile Fourteen reminds me that my right thigh muscle is tight. My shoulders feel the weariness of moving or not moving enough.... I can't figure out which it is. I begin to swing my arms, moving shoulder blades, and this alleviates some of the stress points. For a brief time a woman running near me keeps asking the spectators for Aleve! One runner tells me that "Mile Twenty" is when he heard his entire body grind together and almost snap, and then he moved effortlessly to the end of the race!

In the rhythm of pounding the pavement, I find a space in the movement for prayer! Like on pilgrimage, I lapse into prayers that are rote: the Lord's Prayer; then I begin moving through the Psalms: 121, 23, and 150 pop into mind. I begin to recite the Apostles' Creed, and then start singing Advent songs since today is the second Sunday of Advent. I notice people going to church, dressed fine, sitting in their cars, waiting for us to run by them.

Pilgrimage has been a time for gawking and drinking in the vistas of nature's beauty, and this marathon is no different: I run by amber meadows, large oak trees in winter sparseness, the edge of a brown grassy field, hearing gurgling creeks hidden on the roadside. Gray skies overhead and low clouds, a constant whoosh of a jet flying to the nearby airport.

On this marathon I confront the reality that I am more like Chaucer's merry band of pilgrims than Bunyan's loner: I am greatly heartened by seeing fans on the side of the road. I run by a water table and grab cups of water, and get a jolt of carbs as I grab power bars. The people at the water table give me a "high five," and I smile. I miss running with Lil, the dog, and wish there was someone I knew running with me.

Suddenly, James, a young man in his twenties, runs by my side and begins a conversation: his pregnant wife is running this race as well, though she is behind us. The baby is due in five months, and he is the one who is holding all their power bars. He tells me that he is running just slightly ahead of her because he has to work out all the nervousness of being a young dad.

James falls back to run with his wife, and then "Sixty-Year-Old Man" sidles up to my side. This is his eighth marathon! I tell him that I am impressed, and with that he begins to tell me about all the other marathons he has run.

He slows down, feeling tightness in one of his calves, and then I am joined by Randy. Randy is my age and is a survivor of cancer of the kidneys. He tells me he was running behind me as I shielded him from the cold wind. Randy's family pops up on the side of the road from time to time, holding up a sign that says "You Go, DAD!" and giving him plenty of water and powerbars.

Randy's story is amazing: he had kidney cancer, but it is in remission. He is running in his first marathon in ten years. In a short span of time, on the open road, we soon become "running buddies." Randy was a godsend, a simple gift of grace. I enjoyed bantering with him along the run, and our conversations soon led us into deeper talks about family life, being a dad, the ups and downs of work, and our Christian faith. We became good companions in a short time and distance. We became committed to the same goal of running across the finish line at the same time, come hell or high water!

The last mile was not to be an easy coast down a hill into the loving embrace of family and friends. Crossing Mile Twenty-Six was all up hill! But Randy and I saw the sign "Finish," and with that sign in sight, we kept each other going, supporting one another, running at the same pace, on the same foot, together. Together we gathered power-bars and more water. Together we shared our lives under a December sun that was just coming out. Companions on the journey, this modern-day pilgrimage, breaking bread, good friendship enjoyed.

As we crossed the finish line together, our respective children ran to our sides, bursting out with "Dad, you did it!" and as we embraced our children, we gave each other a "high five" and laughed as two "old men," our children, and the rest of the runners came to finish the race, the destination, for our modern-day pilgrimage.

Chapter Six

THE UNEXPECTED PILGRIMAGE

The overnight trip to Washington, D.C., was not intended to be a pilgrimage. I planned on a simple "family trip," of the old-fashioned variety, where the parent literally throws the children in the backseat of the big modern car, surrounded by games to play and books to read, and off we would go to a certain destination that only the parent knew. Reminding children in the backseat that "the ride's the thing!" only lasts for the first mile or so; it is soon overtaken by "Are we there yet?" pleas from the backseat drivers.

Fond memories of trips I took with my parents washed over me as we drove north from North Carolina to the nation's capital. I remember the first time seeing the multi-chambered Capitol building, the marble block memorial to Lincoln, and the obelisk honoring Washington. I remember the great expanse of the mall, and the red castle of the Smithsonian collection. When my children arrived on the night before our visit to the capital, we were oohing and aahing over the lights that drew our attention to the noble buildings, statues, and monuments.

We stayed overnight with friends in the l'Arche house in D.C. L'Arche is a Christian community for and with adults with mental retardation and their assistants, part of a worldwide network of such communities. My children were ready to go to bed the moment we poked our heads into one of the houses, and with a quick roll-out of the sleeping bags, we were sound asleep.

The next morning is when we were surprised to find ourselves on a pilgrimage! It began with a simple, unexpected gesture: Mary, one of the assistants who is non-disabled, placed a simple wooden cross on black thread over each of our heads. The cross itself looked like it had been made of twigs from a tree. She had purchased the crosses on a recent trip to Guatemala and wanted to give them to us while declaring that we are pilgrims on this day as we walk around the city. Mary was in the middle of preparing for a trip to Lourdes, France, in the next two days, to go to the cathedral which was to be the focal point of a large pilgrimage of people with disabilities. Many members of this community were wearing T-shirts that shouted to an observer, "PILGRIMAGE" in bright school-bus-yellow colors.

With the crosses around our necks, and the T-shirts shouting "PILGRIMAGE," I finally woke up to realize that I was to take the children on a pilgrimage today! But this was not a pilgrimage of just the sights and sounds of the nation's capital. Instead, this was a pilgrimage of memories: I was being given by God an opportunity to share with my children my childhood memories of going on a trip with my folks (their grandparents), and my brother when I was their age. Not only that: today we would be creating memories as we explored new buildings and exhibits that were not there when I was a child, like the Vietnam Veterans Memorial, or the memorial to the Korean War. What would string all of this together were stories! Stories of my past, stories of our present journey would come together and be as one!

Throughout the day, the children would ask me about the memories of my parents, and memories that I had when I first visited this historic city. I regaled them with stories of visiting a hospital museum that had an embalmed foot of a Civil War general, which I thought was in the Smithsonian. I took them up the Washington Monument, which I still remember walking up. We walked on the side of the reflection pool toward the Lincoln Memorial, stopping along the way to feed the ducks in the pond. We walked into the Museum of American History and reached out to touch the large American flag that was being restored, and we roared at the mammoth elephant in the Natural History Museum next door.

But we also made new memories that day, visiting the Holocaust museum, and listening to the stories of those people who had been killed during the horrible days of Hitler's reign. We walked to the Vietnam Veterans Memorial, growing silent as we came to the great cut in the earth and touched the marble face with names engraved of those who died in this conflict.

We also visited art galleries, and laughed at some of the sculpture that was in an outside garden. We stood in line to get into the IMAX show in the Air and Flight Museum, wishing we were birds, or flying in a hot air balloon, or in a biplane, skimming the Grand Canyon's Colorado River.

Our day ended with an ice cream cone and memories of a beautiful day in the city. The sun was setting as we sat underneath one of the cherry trees blossoming overhead. It was a pilgrimage through boyhood memories, stories of the past with my parents and brother, given to the next generation to savor and share with their children. In an action-packed day, with new photos and stories, blending with old stories and rich memories, the next generation will inherit the stories for the pilgrimage of a family that moves onward to tomorrow, but remembering always today and the past of yesterdays.

Chapter Seven

HOLY ISLAND BITTER

There comes a point in reading a plethora of stories of far-away travel by the likes of Paul Theroux and Rick Steves, whetting my appetite for pilgrimage through foreign lands to places like Santiago de Compostela, Rome, and Jerusalem, that I fall into temptation. I have to go and explore the very place itself, or a place a little bit out of the ordinary in a "foreign land." The travel writer's prose gives off that mystical, almost seductive wiggling crook of the index finger while he whispers a "come closer" invitation, and I ache to see the historic sights, taste the wine, run to see if the grass is as green and the pilgrimage as authentic as the writer portrays it to be in such vivid, bold, and dramatic colors.

Such was the case with going to Lindisfarne — the "Holy Isle" — located at the most northeastern part of England, on the rustic southern rural border of Scotland, less than an hour away from Edinburgh. I knew of Lindisfarne from reading the Venerable Bede's tales of the lives of St. Aidan and St. Cuthbert, and I wanted to see, touch, listen, walk, be still, be silent, in solitude in this holy place where, once upon a time, miracles magically unfolded like large blossoms and were as numerous as weeds in a springtime meadow. Spiritual romance was in the air.

On a Tuesday night, with little time for a smooth transition from a whirring life, I abruptly disentangled myself from my relationships of family and friends in North

Carolina, departing from Raleigh-Durham International Airport in a sleek silver jet to London's modern, suburban, out-of-the-way Gatwick International. I am learning that pilgrimage is a time to disentangle myself from some relationships so that I can be surrounded by the mystery that awaits me.

After arriving in London, visiting the cavernous Canterbury Cathedral and the smaller Dorchester Abbey on the Thames, once-home to St. Birinus, I follow a line of traffic between Oxford and Lindisfarne. I join a throng of weekend tourists heading north, too many sheep to count, passing baronial estates that remind me of *Brideshead Revisited,* but no pilgrims walking or hitchhiking this way. Traveling from south to north, I drive the M1 and A1 highways through the industrial heart of nineteenth-century England, glancing by Manchester, driving passed Derbyshire and Newcastle — coal country — which has an enormous angel on a hill near the motorway, standing a good five to six stories high, her wingspan almost equal, a brown, rusted work of contemporary metal art, watching us motorists as we zoom toward Newcastle proper, with tourists looking like little people near her enormous iron feet.

Bright sunshine greeted me on my entrance to the Holy Isle, otherwise known as Lindisfarne. The tide is out so I could drive across the dry road. When the tide is in, it is impossible to drive on the road, as Lindisfarne becomes the Holy Isle. I drive past shallow ocean bed and sweeping sand dunes before I come to a slight rise in the road and drive into town. The town is huddled together among a handful of roads that cross each other, with no traffic light to be found. No building is more than two or three stories high, and most of the buildings are made of fieldstone, brick, or whitewashed stucco or plaster of some kind. It is a quaint English village, complete with a pub, The Ship, and Lindisfarne castle off in the distance, unapproachable this day because of the signs that read "No Entrance: Foot and Mouth Disease Contaminated Area." The sheep in the area are all marked on their fat rumps with either blue stain or red stain. They will be slaughtered because of this horrible disease. A fieldstone wall keeps them fenced in and us fenced out. They bleat as I walk by, but I dare not get close. Even the English Heritage Center, which holds the story of Lindisfarne, is closed due to the disease. On March 20, St. Cuthbert's feast day, a statue of St. Cuthbert was to be placed in the middle of the priory ruins of the Benedictine Abbey on the Holy Isle, but the plan has been scrapped because of the disease.

Few tourists gather on this day on this raw, windy shoal of land. Many of those who do come are bird watchers, as this area has been marked off as a natural wildlife preserve. The main industry is tourism, followed by fishing, with shepherding a distant "last place." In the "off season," which must be now, there are only 160 people who live here. One extended family boasts that all three generations live here. I believe there are more people in the cemetery than there are among the living population of the Holy Isle.

I walk out toward the castle until I can go no further. The castle is on a rocky promenade, jutting out in the churning gray-green ocean, on a slight rise, overlooking Lindisfarne to the west and the North Sea to the east. I listen effortlessly to the pervasive deafening silence, only to hear out of the silence the small waves gurgling and lapping on rocky or sandy shores, a tern-like bird skipping-running across an incoming wake of water. Children play nearby, kicking a ball, a soccer ball, in the field near St. Mary's, the Anglican church. Wild daffodils give a bright splash of yellow edging to the gray fieldstone church.

The church is chilly inside, and even the priest wears a coat. The fieldstone walls on the outside are the very same fieldstone walls on the inside. In other words, there is no insulation. Built in the nineteenth century, this jewel of a church, with its old wooden pews and worn stained-glass windows, is now part of the rock formation of the Holy Isle. My hunch is that it will always stand, or else be in competition with the relic of the Benedictine priory for "Best Falling Apart Ruin on Holy Isle."

The Benedictine priory is a rusty red and earthy brown stone shell of its former self. Kelly green grass grows where pews and tables once stood. This shell is a large communal tombstone amid the plethora of smaller, ancient tombstones and marble markers. A marker placed by the English Heritage Society identifies it as a historic relic. I almost trip over the stones and markers running between the priory and the church, as they are sprinkled over the grass, dotting the ground as if they were children playing underneath the skirts of these two large standing buildings.

In the middle of the expansive graveyard, near a B&B that abuts the cemetery, is St. Aidan's statue. Aidan's statue will continue his lone vigil for a little while longer because of the disease. He holds his greenish-brass shepherd's rod in his right hand, and a stone Celtic cross looms over his head. Aidan came here as a missionary, sent from the Iona community, by way of a monastery at Riveleaux. It is Aidan who baptized the Norse King Oswald of this area in the sixth century. And it was a vision of Aidan himself, being lifted to the heavens by God's angels over the waters, that startled the next bishop of the Holy Isle, Cuthbert, a mere boy watching over sheep on the Holy Isle . . . and nothing was ever the same again for the young shepherd.

Not too far from the church when the tide is out it is possible to walk across the rocky tidal basin to a smaller isle that was St. Cuthbert's burial plot, before he started the journey between York and Durham Cathedral. When the Norse raiders invaded this isle, the Benedictine monks scurried off with the intricately carved wooden coffin of Cuthbert, going north and south along the shoreline and inland, until he came to his final resting place at Durham Cathedral. I walk out the next day through the rocks and climb the slight rise and behold the vastness of the land and the panoramic view of endless, fathomless turning sky around me. I am dizzy from trying to take it all in. It is too much sky and not enough land to root oneself. The vista is dramatic or an English country landscape, depending on which way you look. Looking to the west, to the smooth coastline, I see a passenger train lit up like a line of small Christmas tree lights hugging the coastline, traveling north, with a lingering cloud of smoke following, a rainstorm sweeping over the land like a wedding veil. On the eastern shore of the isle, toward the North Sea, there is the serene calm beauty of a picture postcard blue sky, the absence of clouds drawing attention to itself. In between, like the stuffing of sandwich with wind as bread, I am blown about by the swiftly tilting, changing currents of air. At one moment, the wind is in my face, and then it switches to my side, almost punching me to the ground. It is no wonder why the trees fail to grow tall here as the wind naturally prunes them all to a stubby proportion.

During the two evenings I am in Lindisfarne, I go next door to The Ship. It is here I find my modern-day "pilgrims" as I drink pints of Holy Island Bitter. In the dark wood confines of this pub I meet Louise, a clergywoman in the Anglican Church who has just been moved by her bishop.

She and her husband come and stay a night or two in The Ship pub and inn once every six months. Louise told me that I should go to St. Winifred's in Wales, which has the magic well, a source of healing powers. Louise is an amateur archeologist, which is what also attracts her to this place as she finds bits and pieces of Delft China plates, saucers, and cups on the beach, relics of centuries past. I never did find out much about Roy, her husband. He just smiled at me benignly.

The Ship's owner and I become quick friends as I enjoyed "pub grub" meals there, from breaded-and-fried fish and chips, to a truly English hot meal of roast beef, Yorkshire pudding, potatoes, and peas, always accompanied by a pint or two of Holy Island Bitter. I tried Lindisfarne Meade, but thought it tasted like sweet, alcoholic sugar water. For me, the drink of choice is Holy Island Bitter. I nurse my bitter, slipping slowly into the pub culture, and listen in on the stories of the other pilgrims in this place, which once was home to pilgrimage. Dionne Warwick is singing in Muzak rhythms in the background over the small black-boxed Bose speakers attached to the compact disk player, asking me the strange question: "Do you know the way to San Jose, I've been away so long?" a queer question to ask me in Lindisfarne. Two women sitting by me, their silvery gray hair shining in the pub lights, eat their fish and chip platters while smoking and chattering, giggling, and guffawing at points, interrupted by "Y'don't saaaay?" They fondly embrace each other before they leave this evening to their respective homes. The accent tonight is not from Oxford, Canterbury, or London. The pub owner tells me it is a northern accent, part Scots, as I am less than sixty miles from Edinburgh. Suddenly two black labs, their coats velvety smooth, prance in, their owner soon behind. They belong to an old fisherman, one of the few who can make a living at this business of fishing. His salty disposition is matched by his salt and pepper hair. These are the type of "pilgrims" like Chaucer's lot, except the place of destination is the warm kindly embrace of the pub and the pub owner.

For two days I walk the earth that is the place of holy feet. I had read for several classes Venerable Bede's account of the lives of St. Aidan, St. Cuthbert, and King Oswald. I go to Sunday morning Eucharist at St. Mary's of the Holy Island Anglican church to worship God at this small but still alive church. I walk around the isle again, all Sunday afternoon and early evening, snapping photos of the sky and sun that is as richly, thickly textured as any of Vincent Van Gogh's paintings of the sky during the day or evening. The great presence of the sun looks like Van Gogh filled his brush with a blob of orange, another glob of red, and hint of yellow-gold on the bristles, and swirled it again and again on the bare canvas. While the paint was still wet, the artist then took his thumb and smeared it from that center point outward, extending the rays of orange-gold to the thick blackened cloud. Then, with more orange, sometimes red, and now a touch of pink, oil paint turned into watercolored wash, the artist highlights everything that is on the landscape with wet paint as the setting sun makes all the world around me glisten and shine and makes a cathedral of the sky.

That evening, after I take a bath, I follow a strange impulse and go out to the graveyard, wearing a Polartec fleece vest and raincoat. The rickety wooden fenced gate that is usually open is closed and curiously locked. I sit on the gate itself, swinging my legs to and fro like a small child, and peer into the cemetery until my eyes are used to the darkness. A small blue searchlight from a fishing boat in the harbor swings and casts a steady beam around the grounds every twenty seconds, glancing off the cemetery's inhabitants. For a moment I feel like I am in the middle of the cemetery scene from Thornton Wilder's *Our Town*. It is here that I talk to the saints and souls about the reason for this pilgrimage. "Thanks for bringing me here Aidan, Cuthbert, and Oswald," I say matter-of-factly, assuming they are listening. I thought it only fair to start off with a note of gratitude to the saintly presence. But then I turned my questions into an interrogation because of the nagging feeling that I had wasted my time in coming all the way up here. I mean, where on this rocky shoal are the other pilgrims? My voice begins to rise. I start to spit out my anger and anguish, believing that someone, somewhere, will answer:

> Why'd you bring me up here? I've been to a lot more active places of holy pilgrimage. The only possible pilgrims I can find are the people in the pub, and possibly two women who look like nuns from some monastic order, in their light blue dresses and white head coverings, who aren't the least bit friendly or kind. Where are the other pilgrims? Lost? All I can find are a bunch of bird watchers.

Silence. I listen deeply to the silence. Reflection. It begins to dawn on me that this incredible impulse to get out of the warm bath and sit on the cold fence is itself an interesting stirring that led me to sit on the gate, in the silence of a full night, and listen to God. The white inky moon hovers overhead as my companion.

Like the doors of the dam that are rusted closed from time and lack of use, now suddenly open from the inside, with the increasing force of the water behind the stuck doors pushing me, flooding over, benign inquisition and stagnant creativity give way to revelation and uncontrolled discovery.

Christian pilgrimage is not something we can or have to create, but is a performing gesture we inherit from those who are traveling with us as members of the holy communion of saints, and whose stories lead us to the ways of Christ. The way of the pilgrim has already been trod by Jesus Christ himself, whose life, death, and resurrection, his ascension into heaven is done in order that the Paraclete, the Advocate, the Holy Spirit can descend and walk with us, showing us the pilgrim's way to the glorious reign.

On this pilgrimage I'm discovering what makes a pilgrimage a pilgrimage, and what can kill a pilgrimage, or a pilgrimage's holy site, making of it a tourist attraction and historic relic. I realize that while one can be a pilgrim and a tourist, not all tourists are pilgrims. While one can be a pilgrim and on a journey, not all journeys are pilgrimages. What necessitates converting a journey into a pilgrimage is a holy site, with a holy reason for going in the first place. The pilgrim? More times than not, many of us started the pilgrimage without knowing we were on one until some person, some incident, some strange "quirk of life" or what some call "fate" reveals what we didn't know at first or presume possible: that we are on some holy pathway, on a destination to God knows where — literally. In hindsight's 20/20 goggle vision we appreciate the people we've met along the way, and the way they became living signs, symbols, and markers who instruct us as to which way we must go. In hindsight, I should have put up more markers in the past, out of gratitude for momentary glimpses of the pilgrimage vision I saw, but failed to believe in at the time. So blind am I. Or perhaps unbelieving. Or unprepared...unaware...helpless and deaf to the voices of pilgrimage.

Confession: no one in the Methodist or Presbyterian church of my younger years taught me about pilgrimage, mentioned the word "pilgrim," except as a historic factoid related to Plymouth Rock, Thanksgiving, and the naive natives who lived in that region we now call Massachusetts. A Pilgrim was a Puritan, wearing black and gray clothes, with unfashionably big white collars, large black hats, and silver belt buckles on black shiny shoes. In my Protestant upbringing, pilgrimage was not a practice learned, a performed gesture inherited. Rather, many Protestants sit in their churches, ornate or simple, big or small, as if they've arrived at the Holy Land, with their pew, their seat, reserved for years on end, with no one else allowed to sit in their coveted spot. In the American colonial period, wealthy families bought their pew box and had their name engraved upon a gold nameplate. We have forgotten that the earliest followers of Christ were called people of "the Way" (Acts 9:2)). Today we are people of "the Sit."

Participating in worshiping God in Christ in Roman Catholic churches more frequently lately, I am slightly buoyed when I hear the priest remind us that the church is a "pilgrim church," though only a few people have a clue as to the costly grace such a title and practice demands of Christians. We are a minority. Nice metaphor; looks real cool on paper curricula for Vacation Bible School or youth rally: "PILGRIMAGE 2001!" "Pilgrimage" is a nice, benign metaphor that lasts a few months, before the next slick advertising campaign.

Still, the question haunts me day and night: what would the church — the body of Christ — look, act, and think like if God's people understood themselves to be inheritors of the practices of the ancient pilgrims of yore? Are we not a people moving inexorably, slouching, running, walking, strolling toward Zion?

The serious practice, the plethora of the necessary, performed gestures of Christian pilgrimage, is — in the best and worse understanding of the term — a "lost art," a craft forgotten in time, a choreographed ballet movement that disappears from our collective consciousness. Is it possible that if the practices of pilgrimage languish, then everything about the artful practice of pilgrimage is lost? It may all very well be true that the art of the pilgrimage, the very crafting of our bodies, minds, and spirits, depends upon a continual, lifelong, community-based, experiential (not experimental) performance of the very gestures that make clear for all to see, hear, and smell, spelling out emphatically that here, these chosen people, this one, is a pilgrim of the risen Christ, as he trips over his own feet responding to the call "Follow me." She walks the walk not out of the joy of singing a silly ditty that sounds like "Merrily we roll along," but because there is no other choice but to respond to the call since all else is indecipherable blather, mumbo-jumbo, and the City of Destruction is consumed by an inferno.

A new feeling and experience on this isle: I had no choice but to move forward on the pilgrim's way, only to turn around at times and see that where I came from no longer made any coherent sense. It was as if the pathway that led me to where I am simply rolled up behind me, leaving no trail, no bread crumbs behind: I had to move ahead. I have talked with immigrant-exiles who tell me how lost they feel when the land they once knew and called home no longer exists because of political reasons: they had to move forward. Personally, I know friends who have left a church or a seminary because of what I call a "conspiracy of theological thuggery." Their careers and lives have been nearly destroyed because of the immoral practices of the church: they traveled onward.

The way ahead has a banner over it, tied to two twin poles saying "Fear-Excite." To walk ahead is fraught with fear, the "I'm scared" impulse, but ringed with enough excitement to stimulate nerve and synapse as the foot goes forward. Walking sticks stand idly by in a bucket by the entrance of our baptism. Certain stops ahead for Eucharist — nourishment of body, mind, and spirit — are promised. Ahead, as I walk onward I am purified in the exceedingly bright lightness of it all as I walk forward, yet grow weak, but my senses are made sharper than ever by the cutting-edge, polishing-stone life we leave behind. Within the pilgrim is a speck of holy fire clinging to my bleeding, pumping heart.

I am aware that I have been plunged into hot-house moments of pilgrimage, in places of incredible beauty, with pilgrims whose broken-boned lives, bandaged blistered feet, soaring songs of Christian agony, and veneration before holy icons have unleashed primal moods. My greatest hidden fears are exposed before Corpus Christi hanging black, nailed, and bloodied on the roughly hewn cross. "Take, eat, this is my body" intones the baritone priest, handing it out to me to consume and be consumed. I am surrounded by a gaggle of bewildered and desperate Marys and fearful disciples by the score in small chapels. "It is shed for you, for you, take it from my hands now, for the forgiveness of your sins, Brett, which are countless as the stars," I quietly remind myself. "Amen" we mutter reverently with hurting egos, brittle lives, which are utter failures and yet are saved when we admit "I can't do it on my own anymore. My success is my own custom-made charade."

A burst of enthusiasm propels me forward as I rush the next morning to Durham, throw money into the parking meter, leap up stairs, and run into the cathedral. I grab a map of the interior of the cathedral and pinpoint

St. Cuthbert's and the Venerable Bede's graves and markers on the map. While I have been to Durham's cathedral before as tourist, this time I go as if it were an insatiable need. I quietly jog down the length of the chancel, running toward the altar, and go behind the altar to an area with a large wooden canopy overhead and a large stone slab marked "CUTHBERTUS" in medieval capital letters. I collapse on my knees on the small padded kneeling bench in front of his grave, read the prayer written and stamped on the kneeling bench, and then in hushed tones thank God for the life of Cuthbert in showing me the difference between tourist and pilgrim, journey and pilgrimage. And for the pilgrimage Cuthbert made in his life for the glory of God, I give God the glory. In the small museum, the two women who run the operation give me freedom to go and see the actual intricately carved coffin of St. Cuthbert. The figure of the Christ, the Apostles, and the four gospel writers are squeezed onto the coffin's surface. Relics of crosses and combs from the coffin are on display. Four hundred years after he died, carried through York, Durham, and Lindisfarne, the falling-apart coffin was opened, only to reveal Cuthbert's body not only intact, but as "fresh as the day he died." I run to Bede's coffin and again fall on my knees before his tomb and thank God for Bede and his biography of Cuthbert, whose story shows the great length we are called to go as pilgrims of the most High.

As I leave through the heavy wooden doors of Durham Cathedral it dawns on me: today is March 20, the feast day of St. Cuthbert. I smile a knowing smile as my pilgrimage has brought me to the resting place of the pilgrim Cuthbert.

In the small English village of Caythorpe, outside of Nottingham, my old friends the Banks welcome me with open arms, a lunch of hot soup, a beer, and tea and scones.

We take a long meandering walk along the road outside their home, with dollops of daffodils springing out of the ground, walking down to see one of the oldest tin churches still standing in England, painted pretty in pink. These tin churches were built at the turn of the last century. It happens to be "St. Aidan's." Again, I smile that smile that knows this is more than "sheer coincidence," "happenstance," or "dumb luck." Providence chose this day and smiles with me at my discovery. After all, I was not expecting to be at Cuthbert's tomb when I arranged this trip some months before. Durham was not on my agenda. I did not plan on spending a moment in a quaint country church named for St. Aidan. My pilgrim's path and the path of the pilgrims who lived before me, yet whose story resides in my bones, are entwined and are becoming one. Do I have the faith to live the pilgrim's life? Or is it the gift of faith by grace that has led me safely to visit the resting places of my brothers Bede and Cuthbert in order that I may have confidence of my convictions of faith?

The next morning I board the plane in Manchester. I feel the relationship which means the world to me start to be on my mind as the plane descends into Raleigh-Durham International Airport. This time of pilgrimage in England is now over. But the time of pilgrimage is always a time of grace unfolding as I understand better the way my life in its entirety is a pilgrimage just begun, to places in the world, and in my life, that have not yet been touched. Pilgrimage happens through places, among people, and over time. Pilgrimage occurs even when standing in place, as I walk carefully and mindfully the curious ways of my life. Before me and within me lies the pilgrim's way, which is more mystery than I know what to do with. I look forward to a pint of Holy Isle Bitter from time to time.

Chapter Eight

FOLLOW ME

Based upon the success of the first class of graduate students who went on pilgrimage, I took another class of thirteen students on another pilgrimage. This pilgrimage involved going a slightly different route in a more rural part of North Carolina. What I would come to discover in this pilgrimage is that the same impulse that propelled and guided the first group of graduate students came to the surface again with this group of students. By the end of their journey, the students had been changed into a gathering of pilgrims.

Before the pilgrimage began, we gathered in an old farmhouse in a rural county and began with an evening prayer. Sister Stef, a Benedictine sister, read the students a story of pilgrimage that set the tone of the pilgrimage:

> You have to walk across a moor. You set out from a well-lighted house in which you have looked at maps and been given instructions. You start off on the track. As you walk on, dusk falls and it is more difficult to see the way. Then it is completely dark. You cannot see your direction, and it is so cloudy that you cannot even see whether you are still on the path — or even whether there is a path. But you stumble on, hoping you are going in the right direction. Then a thunderstorm comes on and the going is even rougher. But just now and then there is a flash of lightning, and though

it lasts only for a fraction of a second it is just long enough for you to see that your feet are on the track.[1]

I reminded the students that on our pilgrimage, we sometimes do not see much more than the step before us. The lightning of life itself becomes a tool of God's grace, lighting up only slightly the step before us in the darkness. It is enough light, though, to lure us forward to our destination, which is God.

We slept in the coolness of the farmhouse in sleeping bags, some nervous about the challenge before us of going on pilgrimage. This was more than a walk through the countryside: with a six-foot cross before us as we walked along over fifteen miles, the challenge before us was obvious: while most seminary courses are taught and conducted in classrooms where everyone gets to sit, this was a classroom on the road of life, where everyone participated in learning the practices, the rituals, the prayers, the songs of pilgrimage.

The next morning we all collectively woke up bright and alert at seven o'clock! People were responsible for getting their own breakfast, with Bill, one of the pilgrims, making it clear: "No good coffee, no pilgrimage!" Showered, shaved, and having collected all our gear and food for the journey, we shoved off for our pilgrimage.

At ten o'clock, we are at our pilgrimage starting-off point. We have hats on our heads, tennis shoes, sun block, and fanny-packs. Cely, one of the students, provides for each person a gift of a necklace with a clay cross she made in the shape of a Jerusalem cross. I give instructions for the journey: first, follow the cross! No one can go before the cross in the walk. The cross leads the way. Second, walk

---

1. Dame Maria Boulding, "Prayer and the Paschal Mystery," *Downside Review* 94, no. 317 (1976): 284.

single file on the open road, walking against the flow of traffic. Lastly, do not wave back at people or respond to them while we are walking as that could cause an accident. With cars zooming by us at fifty-five miles per hour, the last thing we needed was an accident. I shouted "Formation!" and off we went!

Mile One: In this first mile, the unexpected moments of pilgrimage's lessons began to unfold among us: a white-haired gentleman in his eighties slows down in his beat-up old red Chevy. A solitary crucifix hangs from his rearview mirror. He bows deeply and sincerely, making the sign of the cross, pointing at our cross and his cross on the mirror, smiling, and moves on. We will see him later in the afternoon when he crosses paths with us again, this time with his grandson, asking, "What are you doing?" Bill answered "We are on Christian pilgrimage!" And the elder said, "I thought so!" with a knowing smile, thumbs-up, bowing again slightly, smiling broadly, and off he went in his car, waving good-bye.

Mile Two: The students feet are learning the walk of pilgrimage! We are aware of how tenderfooted we are as we are experiencing new sensations, aches, blisters, and aching shoulders, all in the first two miles. The body learns the art of pilgrimage at this time.

Mile Three: An appetite! People are getting hungry, now enjoying bananas and water. We are starting to put on more sun screen as the sun's warmth continues to grow in intensity.

Our line, while still single-file, is now spreading out. While we had much energy at the beginning of the journey, after three miles some people are starting to slow down while others keep up the initial pace. This works well as the groups of three or four people have time to walk *and* talk with one another, getting to know one another better on this pilgrimage.

Mile Four: We walked a mile in silence and prayer. What is always interesting about this time of silence is that people actually move quicker when they are not talking; there is more uniformity to the line, and the silence, while awkward at first, soon becomes a comforting presence as the inner pilgrimage — the pilgrimage into the depths of our souls — starts to take on a force of its own. In a sense the "outward" walk provides a way that the pilgrim can be on an inner walk, exploring matters of the heart in the silent yet rhythmic pace of the walk itself.

Mile Five: We are reminded that this is the "South" and is a land of history as we walk by the town of Pittsboro, North Carolina's statue honoring and memorializing the fallen Confederate States of America soldiers on the court house square.

Unlike the other pilgrimage with students, which included all white men, our pilgrimage this year includes women, including one African American woman, and this seems to have made a difference in the reactions of those who are driving by or stopping on a sidewalk to stare at us. No comments or queries about our pilgrimage like there were the year before.

Mile Eight: We are now walking in the country. There are undulating hills, gurgling brooks that are hidden in the hills and small dales along the roadside. I look carefully in the middle of the fields to our right and left as deer are known to sleep there from time to time.

Mile Nine: We begin to adorn the cross we are carrying with meaningful debris and flowers we find on the side of the roadway. We weave the branch that was used for the reaffirmation of the baptismal covenant along the arm of the cross, while bottle tops, small stones, forsythia branches with yellow flowers peep out from the myriad branches on the cross.

Mile Ten: The cross is now festooned with memories as it is filled with material that is meaningful for each pilgrim. I am walking in the very far back of the pack, and I am struck by the scene before me: a group of people walking in single file behind the cross of Christ. The cross is held high over the head of the person carrying it. It is an incredibly humbling scene to watch this parade of pilgrims before me.

The conversations by this time of our journey start to be a sharing not only of the stress on our bodies, but a sharing of the stories of the various pilgrimage narratives we have read for over a semester. We remind one another of books, stories, movies, paintings, and music we have heard over the course of a semester that reminds us that we are but the latest group of pilgrims on this earthly journey, whose desire is to proclaim Christ as we walk with Jesus on this gorgeous day. The Holy Spirit is present, touching us in meaningful ways as we take the opportunity to engage in conversation people with whom we have not spent much time during the semester.

Mile Twelve: Like on the journey to Chimayo, we doff our caps and hats at Christian churches and cemeteries. In this part of the South, there are small cemeteries in innocuous places, in which the tombstones reveal that people were buried in these plots of land over the nineteenth century, and were usually African American. These cemeteries are close to the white churches, but not too close.

We walk by a small African Methodist Episcopal Zion church, a one-story, simple brick building, home to an

African American congregation. Up the road a ways is a large, red brick, stately, United Methodist church, home to a white congregation. Both Methodist, yet segregated because of race: a living reminder of that which still divides the church, namely, race.

Mile Thirteen: Do animals understand that we are on pilgrimage, or near the end of the pilgrimage? It seems to be a common experience that when I get close to finishing a pilgrimage cats, dogs, horses in pens near the end of the journey, even cows, move over to the group of pilgrims, making much noise and commotion. Who is alerting the animals to the presence of pilgrims? God?

Mile Seventeen: In the air there is a sense of satisfaction and hope as people walk the last mile of the pilgrimage. We began at ten o'clock; it is nearing five o'clock. The line of pilgrims is strung out, people trying to take that one more step, which is a constant and conscious effort at this point. One young woman, who has had problems with her legs for years, feels her knee pop out. She stops, massages the knee into place, and tells us all that she is going to finish this pilgrimage on her own steam, so get out of the way!

The Journey's End: We all arrive at different times, but we all wait for one another in the inner gate of the farmhouse where we all slept the night before. One by one the pilgrims saunter in and immediately sit down. We pray the prayer of the pilgrims at journey's end, praying that "the Lord of heaven and earth, who so graciously accompanied us on this pilgrimage, continue to keep us under his protection."

We finished the journey for the day, but the journey continues onward for each of the pilgrims. We remind ourselves that we are to simply "follow Jesus," following the one who

137

calls us on our earthen pilgrimage to "Follow me!" After a pilgrimage, the imperative, "Follow me!" has new meaning as we each take up our cross daily and follow Christ. The collective of individuals who began the course four months earlier has become a band of pilgrims, a Christian community, who, through the challenge of an actual pilgrimage, now draw closer together as disciples of the risen Christ, who continues to call us to "Follow me!"

Chapter Nine

PERSEVERING PURGATORY

In the middle of the ancient, rugged, massive green island of Ireland, straddling the political border between the "Troubles" of Northern Ireland and the semi-autonomous Republic of Ireland, a few miles outside the small village of Pettigo in County Donegal, is the windswept island known as St. Patrick's Purgatory. Called by its haunting name — Purgatory — the island is surrounded by slate gray waters that are never still but constantly churning. Purgatory is in the middle of a large, dark lake — Lough Derg — surrounded by the undulating forested hills and wide open skies, a cauldron for churning clouds.

Legend has it that Ireland's St. Patrick walked the barren, largely unpeopled land nearby, perhaps spending time alone in prayer and penance upon a nearby small island known as Saints Island, or the larger Station Island. Because of St. Patrick's mere presence here in 445 and later England's King Owen's pilgrimage to this island in 1140, people have followed their footsteps for a thousand years as a mystical pilgrimage of cleansing, of penance. The hope that draws people is that they will not need to go through such a highly stringent and austere penance again in "the afterlife" in order to reach heaven's gates. Pilgrimage on this island was enough like purgatory to placate a rather vengeful and fiery God of justice. Without *this* Purgatory, God would otherwise stop us on the glorious heavenly toll road from entering through Heaven's Gates until our dirty lives had been thoroughly scrubbed and cleansed.

Today, St. Patrick's Purgatory is open for three-day pilgrimages from June 1 to August 15 every year. While an amazing eleven thousand people went on pilgrimage in 2001, the records show that up to thirty thousand people went on pilgrimage on any single year in the 1950s. To foster such devotion again, the priests of St. Patrick's Purgatory have launched a public relations campaign, with posters and media blitz that herald "Lough Derg Break: Time for Body and Soul."

I flew into Ireland on a Thursday, July 12, a day that the "Troubles" of Northern Ireland are either celebrated or feared, depending solely upon where one lives and if one is Catholic or Protestant. Over the radio news stations I heard that nearby Armagh was braced for violent clashes today between Ulster Unionists and a radical fringe of the IRA. Renting a car in Dublin, I traveled north to Pettigo during the evening rush hour. In Kell I took a photo of a beautiful large statue of the Virgin Mary in the center of town as a reminder of all the smaller statues of Mary set into small booths on the roadside. Further down the road I remember a nonchalant British soldier waving me through one of the border crossings of Northern Ireland. On my right was a Protestant church with two flags flying upon its turreted stone tower: one flag was for the British, and the other flag was orange for the Protestants — or Proddies as I heard them, including myself, called. Opposite the church, on a street light pole, was a poster for a candidate from the Sinn Fein political party — a political party usually connected with the IRA and known for its Catholic roots and anti-British stance. A few miles later I came upon a life-size statue of two figures embracing one another with the words,

"PEACE FOR ALL" etched on its circular base. In Enniskillen I drove under a colorful banner that hung over the street proclaiming "God Save the Queen": the police station is surrounded by a yards of black wire mesh fence, looking like a military command post.

The further north I wander, the more the land resembles a lush green carpet of old evergreen and deciduous trees, green and yellow vegetation growing on open farming meadows, and white sheep with black muzzles everywhere. Dotting the land were small whitewashed stone houses with bold-colored doors. Pettigo sits precariously on the border between these two countries. I met a police office in Pettigo as I drove into town who asked me if I had any meat or dairy product: "Fear of mad cow disease," said the police. Hearing my American accent, he waved me on.

The bed and breakfast where I planned to spend the evening had let my room go to another guest by mistake, so I was set up with Mary at her farmhouse, "The Carne." Mary was a widow — her husband died of a heart attack when he was fifty-two — living most of her adult years in this large house, raising four children without a father. The house was surrounded no longer by cows but by large trees, wild green grass, and a magnificent garden in full bloom, all at their summertime high of growing. Mary had returned this morning from a pilgrimage to Lourdes, France, yet had enough vim and vigor to feed me a great breakfast of Kellogg's Corn Flakes, Wheetabix cereal, fresh milk, sausage, bangers, tomatoes, bacon, eggs-over-easy, tea, toast and jam at 10:00 in the evening. Mary herself has been on the pilgrimage of St. Patrick's twelve times: "If you go on pilgrimage three times, legend has it that you then don't have to go to Purgatory, but straight to heaven." In her generous hospitality, I found that this Mary embodied the very virtues of Mary the mother of God.

Rested, I bounded downstairs in the morning, ready for breakfast. But I stopped abruptly when I remembered: "I'm to begin fasting today." Slowly I walk upstairs to the bathroom and begin to shave, drink water, do some sit-ups and push-ups, and leave Mary's house. Knowing I'm Protestant, she points out that just over the hill from her house is the Carn Graveyard, "one of the few cemeteries here where both Catholic and Protestants are buried side-by-side."

Driving along a winding country road, hemmed in by rugged hillside green hedges, I come to an abrupt clearing: directly in front of me is a large metal arch bearing the words "Saint Patrick's Purgatory." There is a small, ornate chapel on my left, and a boathouse toward the water's edge, with two boats or jetties tied up at the pier. Many cars are parked in the car lot. Two women are sitting on a bench near the boat, waiting to go to the island. Anticipation mounts.

Next to the chapel is a smaller building where I pick up my room and bunk assignment and pay my twenty-five pounds for the trip over to the sacred isle: 103A is my bunk in a building that looks like any college dorm in the States. I am handed a small pamphlet that tells me all I will need to know for the next few days: when the dining hall is open for my one meal a day; when we go to sleep; a small map of the places around the island; and the busy schedule of worship — Mass — and when to "work" or walk the Stations on the Penitential Beds. To sum it up, I will complete nine Stations in my bare feet over three days while fasting on a diet of cold toast, black tea or black coffee (no milk), with a twenty-four-hour vigil stuck in between all the activities for good penitential measure. The medieval pilgrims would come here for pilgrimage for fifteen days before their vigil even began, when the pilgrim was locked in a cave with nothing but water to drink. I smile, intrigued by the daunting barefoot pilgrimage before me, including a twenty-four-hour vigil, shaking my head, wondering how I bumped or fell into this pilgrimage site.

I climbed into the blue boat with two women from Cork, who have walked on this isle nine times, and one woman from Killkenny, who has been here twenty times. None of them have ever come with their husbands. Many women come here with a friend or two expressly without their husbands or children for a "quiet weekend away." There are far more women — young and old alike — than men on the isle. I am told by some women that this is due to the roles of women and men in modern Irish society: women are expected to be more religious than men. Yet I found among many of the men, and some young people, that they come to get some perspective — a godly vantage point — on their lives and the world in which we live. I laughed out loud when one young person went so far as to call this "fun" as she enjoyed chatting and getting to know new people over three days and many miles.

The five-minute boat ride brings us to the concrete pier of the almost treeless isle. There is only one large tree that stands as witness to the many pilgrims in the middle of the Penitential Beds. As I walk off the boat, the first building I come to is a shop of religious souvenirs next to the smaller Gothic chapel of St. Mary's. In 1870, the larger Romanesque St. Patrick's Basilica was built, replacing this smaller chapel for all religious services. The basilica has a high copper-turned-green roof and Celtic cross that dominate the island's squat landscape.

Wide open for the adventure before me, a residue of tiredness still resting on my shoulders, I stroll over to the men's dormitory, following the women. Going up to the second floor of the men's dormitories, I walk into a large room that has been neatly divided by room dividers into small cubicles. In each cubicle are two sets of bunk beds. Leaving my bags by the side of my bunk, I watch other men who quickly take off their street shoes, Doc Martin boots, or Adidas running shoes, and socks, sliding the pair under their metal bunks. I sit down and do the same. Tenderly and with trepidation about the cold I will meet outside, I walk down the stairs to the cool, sunny outdoors. The soles of my soft feet touch the hard wet pavement. I never thought so much about the feet of pilgrims. The stripping of shoes and socks soon after one arrives raises awareness of the feet. For a moment I stand and watch clouds, trying to guess if a rain-filled storm cloud was coming. I watch others walk by, some wearing North-face parkas, others with their button-up beautiful hand-knit sweaters or cardigans; a woman walks by in a fur-collared coat, nursing a rarely seen white cup of black coffee, while a gentleman in a black Navy wool coat walks quickly by, nodding and muttering, "Good day." Some wear baseball caps; others wear colorful scarves; some wear jeans or nylon sweatpants, while others wear dresses, beautiful skirts, and panty hose.

I was told by Mary at the B&B that the pilgrimage of St. Patrick's Purgatory is a great equalizer of people. It is hard to see — by any outward, ostentatious sign — who is rich or poor, gifted or impaired, college educated professional or housewife, perhaps a stay-at-home father, reasonably healthy or under emotional duress, unless you talk to and enter a relationship with the other person. Those who come are a great cross-section of modern Irish society, whether one is from the Republic of Ireland or Northern Ireland. On this solitary isle we are all pilgrims of God, "working the Stations," as a priest kept reminding us over a period of three days.

Lost about what I do next, for there are no designated guides here, I sit in a pew in the basilica where pilgrims from the previous day are in worship and being guided by a narrative of the Stations of the Cross. An elderly woman who was with me on the ride over to the island taps me on the shoulder and kindly shows me the pattern for this prayer sequence they call a "Station." A Station is a form of prayer that involves physical motion — walking, kneeling, working the rosary, kissing the cross — accompanied by a mantra-type of rote prayer, usually so many "Our Fathers" (without "For thine is the kingdom, and the power"), "Hail Marys," and one (Apostles') Creed. Nine Stations are completed over three days, five around the Penitential Beds, and four in the basilica during the twenty-four-hour vigil. To my naive, Protestant-centric sensibilities, such a rigid discipline is unheard of and unthinkable, and is too good a challenge to pass up: a spiritual boot-camp.

I take out my small pamphlet and begin to follow the instructions carefully. By the end of the ninth Station on the third day, I will know the entire process inside and out. But at my inaugural run at the Station my steps are tentative, full of a spirit of naive bungling, and deep sighing between laughter of embarrassment. Leaving the basilica, I head to St. Patrick's Cross, which is a small cross mounted on a three foot slender stone column. I say one Our Father, one Hail Mary, and one Creed, and then kiss the small iron cross. Then I go to the cross of St. Brigid in the outside wall of the basilica, kneel and say more Our Fathers, Hail Marys, and the Creed. I then stand in front of the cross, and with arms outstretched in the shape of the cross I say publicly, "I renounce the world, the flesh, and the Devil."

Looking at the pamphlet, I walk around the basilica slowly, four times, saying either a decade of the Rosary — which I barely knew — or singing Protestant hymns. I then go up to the first Penitential Bed to St. Brigid and begin my rounds on the Beds.

There are six small Beds that I walk around, saying three Our Fathers, three Hail Marys, and one Creed. I kneel on the thick rock and stone gray wall of a bed and repeat the same mantra-like prayer, and then walk inside the circled bed repeating the sequence of prayers. One more time I recite the prayer sequence, kneeling by a mound inside the circle, upon which a three-foot black metal cross — with corpus — is implanted. The crosses in the six circled mounds look like the Excalibur of Arthurian times: a sword in a stone. Legend has it that each bed used to be a beehive cell which was inhabited by monks from an earlier monastic period. Now they are open rings of sharp-edged boulders and roughly hewn stones embedded up-end in the soil, some on a steep incline, without steps in helping one walk around. One priest jokingly talked about the possibility that other priests come in the middle of the night and physically sharpen the stones as they are not very smooth for a thousand-year-old pilgrimage site. The crucifix in the middle of the mound bears a saint's name: St. Brigid, St. Brendan, St. Columba, St. Patrick, St. Davog, and St. Molaise, each saint having a connection with St. Patrick's Purgatory.

After walking, kneeling, and praying around the Penitential Beds, I go to the lakeside and say seven more Our Fathers, Hail Marys, and one Creed. Then I kneel on a small concrete block on the waters' edge and repeat the sequential prayers. Water laps upon my knees. Finally, I return to St. Patrick's Cross and repeat the prayers, but no kissing this time. I conclude the Station by going into the

basilica alone and recite Psalm 16 to myself: "Protect me,
O God, for in you I take refuge.... You are my Lord, I have
no good apart from you." Completing this intricate pattern
of prayer, walking, kneeling, and kissing crosses takes me
about an hour.

After my first time at the Beds performing a Station, I was
somewhat numbingly bewildered from the experience, never
having prayed so many Our Fathers and Hail Marys or recited the Creed so often — or so fast — in my life. I wasn't
sure if I was "working" the prayers, or if they were working
on me, whatever this meant in this part of the pilgrimage.
I went to the largely empty dining hall and sipped many
cups of coffee and ate numerous slices of dry toast, tasteless
oat cakes, and thick, heavy brown bread in the middle of
the afternoon. The wooden seats in the dining hall were as
hard, wooden, and austere as the pews in the basilica. This
meal is known internationally as the "Lough Derg Meal."
No one else was in the dining hall, and I enjoyed the sweet
sound of silence. I was still wondering how I got here and
trying to remember who told me of this place. I started to
consider some people whom I had offended some time in
my life: ways I failed to listen with more compassion and
interest to my children; failing as a friend to a beloved significant other; not trusting Christ's care in shepherding my
life on this pilgrimage. I was startled from this deepening
reflection by some of the adolescent waitresses who came in
noisily, sitting nearby, chit-chatting among themselves.

Knowing that I had to complete three Stations on the Beds
before 9:00 p.m., I slowly got up from my spot and headed
out to do two more Stations. By the third Station I was con-
fusing Our Father and Hail Marys and the Creed so that it
came out "Our Father who art in heaven, blessed is the fruit
of thy womb Jesus, with whom I believe in the holy catholic

church." I sat down on one of the Beds and started laughing again, this time uncontrollably. "Amen," and I burst out with a roaring laugh. So much for meaningful, pious, romantic, reverential, yet meditative prayer. 'Tis a joy to be human on this island of saints and martyrs.

In between each Station I go into the warm reading room — again, on hard wooden seats — and write in my journal, listening to the Irish brogue spoken naturally around me, and dream about food, shoes, sleep, and a pint of Guinness. I was told that the touch of my shoes, my bedsheets at night, and the taste of food would be heightened by the end of this Pilgrimage.

At 6:15 p.m., the church bell rings for Mass, which begins promptly at 6:30 p.m. A young man at the organ plays beautifully, and the young woman liturgist sings with a clear bell-tone quality to her voice, leading us in singing the Psalms. In the homily a priest describes the hardship of vocation in following Jesus — just like this vigil — citing people like Martin Luther King Jr., Mother Teresa, Gandhi, and Nelson Mandela. As we prepare for Eucharist, the young man at the organ now plays a soulful, melancholy, haunting tune on a long wooden flute. I am in a Celtic wonderland; my heart follows the sad melody of the flute.

Later I shuffle downstairs for the Night Prayer and the Benediction. Outside, it feels almost like winter in North Carolina. The brochure said to bring warm and waterproof clothes: I am layered with clothing for the adventure. A priest whispers to me "The wind in this place makes it colder than it is. One night we went through all four seasons. Dress warmly." At this Night Prayer a large candle near the altar is extinguished because the pilgrimage is over for the one hundred pilgrims who preceded my group of two hundred

pilgrims. A mistake: the organist begins to play Widor's Toc-
cata, a highly celebrative organ composition used in many
weddings. The organist was playing it to celebrate the end
of the vigil for one set of pilgrims. A priest quickly stops the
music, reminding the organist that our group of pilgrims is
at the beginning of the vigil. At the end of the Night Prayers
our group is reminded that we are to break for awhile, but
we are expected to be back by 10:15 p.m. for opening Mass
as the twenty-four-hour vigil is about to begin — just as
all the priests went to bed. The candle is re-lit: our vigil
has begun.

On the first night, the vigil begins at 10:00 p.m. We are
asked to stay awake for twenty-four hours, getting sleep
only on the second night of our stay on the island. Morning and evening Mass are celebrated each day as well as
other liturgies, including the sacrament of reconciliation, reflections on the Stations of the Cross, and reaffirmation of
baptism. There is time for some personal reflection in between the various scheduled parts of the day. There is also a
chance to try "Lough Derg Soup," which consists of salt and
pepper in a cup of hot water, usually consumed at 3:00 a.m.,
in one of the shelters located near the basilica. One shelter,
or rest station, is for the smokers, and a larger one for the
non-smokers.

In one of the shelters, I am befriended by Ronin from
Dublin. In his thirties, Ronin has come to Purgatory four
or five times. Married, his wife expecting their first baby,
Ronin comes here in order to get perspective on God and
on his life, especially as a lawyer in the Dublin area. He gives
me some pointers for doing the pilgrimage inside the basilica throughout the early morning hours. Because there are
no outdoor lights for the Hermits' Beds, we walk the Penitential Stations *inside* the basilica, among the pews, with

a person in front telling us where we would be were we doing the stations outside and what we should be praying and doing throughout the evening. With the quick-tongued guides, I began to say the prayers faster than ever. Among the pointers Ronin gave me — which included walking in a figure-eight pattern around the pews — is the goal of aiming toward the cushioned altar rails whenever it came time to kneel anywhere along the Stations. My knees were sore after the first three Stations outside. By the time I finished three more in the early morning hours, my knees, calves, and thighs throb with life as well as with pain.

What I notice most of all is the uniqueness of the human foot. Like our fingerprint, our eye, the whorls on our big toe, not one foot is the same as any other. It is more than some feet being big or short, thin or wide, pudgy or skeletal. Baring the lonely foot on cold pavement, rocky circles, and marble of the basilica floor, I get to know who is before me and behind me by looking at their feet. On the white flesh of the foot, I notice the purple veins that popped out at the top of people's feet, as well as the small, intricate varicose veins whose plum-colored web spreads along the upper flesh of the foot. Some people have remarkably high arches that you can put half a tennis ball under, while others have the flattest feet, every inch of the sole touching the misty cold pavement.

Feet looked like they had worn out many shoes. Feet at war with shoes misshapen from the pudgy pink, baby-tender foot of one's early years when first learning to walk. Gone the svelte thin feet of youth, with not a blemish or a wrinkle on them, no sign of corns or bunions, or yellowish-white moldy skin, or the scaly crust at the back of the heel. All the toes on one woman's feet were criss-crossing each other,

150

a toe overlapping another toe from years of high heel and stiletto shoes.

Hair on the foot is an intriguing oddity. Some men have absolutely no hair on the knuckles of their toes or the top of the foot, while others have hair that rivals a more primitive beast or past. The hair swirls and splays out, with just a hair or two on the smallest toe. Women as well had hair on toes and the top of feet, the hair sticking out of their nylons. Others shaved the hair off, the dark prickly residue as a reminder of our ancestral, animalistic past. We carry the genes of our Neanderthal and Cro-Magnon past.

I love painted toenails. I distinctly remember one woman whose red toenail polish was chipping during one walk through the Stations. The next time we were walking the Stations, the toenails glistened and glittered with a fresh coat of nail polish. Some wore fire engine red or dark aquatic blue or deadly black; others made patterns with their polish, while some men had clear toenail polish and a half-decent pedicure. One man's toenails were all black.

There are red, angry ingrown toenails, as well as others with a slow-growing, creeping fungus under the nails. Toenails thick and yellow, brittle and antique. Having just finished a course of Lamisil treatment for the fungus, I was only too aware of its presence among my fat hairy toes and unevenly cut toenails. Some people cut their nails close to the pink quick, close enough that it looked like they could bleed, while others had scissor sharp toenails that could hurt if they were even so much as to glance against another person's skin.

12:30 a.m.: the fourth Station. "By St. Brigid's Cross: I renounce the world, the flesh, and the Devil," says the lay reader. We slowly and prayerfully wend our way around the basilica inside as we imitate the walk outside. Being so far north, there is still a hint of daylight glow to the land-scape, even at this early morning hour. The sun begins to peek over the tree tops on the hillside by 5:00 a.m. By the time I finish the Stations in the early morning the prayers and creeds roll off of my tongue almost without intentional effort. All I would do is open my mouth and begin walking "Our Father...." I get a drink of water, my throat is dry, and I sit quietly in one of the shelters near the basilica. My feet are numb. I experience them as cold only if I sit cross-legged or put my baseball cap over the toes and they warm up. The rest of the time I forget about the cold dampness.

It is 2:00 a.m. Now others are flying to the altar rail to kneel on cushions. I fall in front of the lectern, a brass cre-ation, elaborately carved with the story of a pilgrimage in its metal bas relief. "Our Father, who art in heaven...." I'm getting faster with this prayer, seven seconds flat, making it even faster if I use "debts" instead of "trespasses."

Sliding through the prayers, I gaze at the cross of Christ, front and center in the basilica. The top portion of the cross is broken. There is a symbolic rooster at the foot of the cross, jumping out of a black pot. The story goes that there once was a gathering of Roman soldiers seated around a fire, cooking a pot of the remains of a rooster or cockerel, while Jesus is being crucified on the cross. One of the men gathered around the fire says that if the Son of the Virgin has risen, then a rooster would fly out of the pot. And with that dare a rooster flies out of the boiling pot, alive, crowing for all the world to hear!

It is 5:00 a.m. Tired, exhausted, woozy, and swaying whenever I stop moving to kneel. This is the seventh Sta-tion. It is endurance. "Perseverance is a virtue" the church tells us. This is "Pilgrimage Meets Outward Bound," or "Pil-grimage as Survivor Island." It is the coldest temperature of the day; the sun is rising slowly in the east. With the doors of the basilica wide open throughout the vigil, I walk with two layers of coats on, wishing I had sweat pants. People sit in a pew, their heads literally bobbing on the pew — bumpity bump — in front of them as they slumber, or they drift to the side, and — clunk — hit hard on the wooden seat. Awaking suddenly, startled, people loudly blurt forth "Hail Mary, full of grace. . . . "

It is 6:30 a.m. Morning Mass. Father Richard Hoban — the senior priest — leads worship, no music at this hour. The group preceding our group looks refreshed. I am envious of their sleep. This is a heck of a way to learn the virtue of perseverance. I fall asleep during Mass. Behind me, a finger in my side — I am poked awake. Is this the virtue of charity?

Some people heard — through my accent — that I was from the States, and was the lone Protestant. In talking to people on this isle, I have to ask people to repeat, their brogue so thick and almost unintelligible. Invariably, the question turns to "Why are you here?" I quickly turn it back on them: "Why are *you* here?" and they smile. It opens up conversation quickly.

The reason that many are here is because the pilgrimage affords them the opportunity to be more "themselves" than any other time or place in their busy lives. This is most profound during the sacrament of reconciliation. Each person is welcomed to come to the altar and confess their sins to one of the priests. As they go in, I — the Protestant — go to the Beds and begin working on the eighth Station. One by one, I am joined by other pilgrims who have finished their confession. I feel like we are ants, scrambling over the stones and rocks, each working the prayer at our individual pace, trying to work the penance out of these Penitential Beds. We work the prayers as they work us. The prayers work on more than our minds, our bodies move, limb and foot, with tired, cold fingers we grab the edge of a Bed wall, learn to move with other bodies without tripping over each other. Am I spiritually refreshed? I am too physically and mentally exhausted to know.

As the body weakens from tiredness, the more open we are to ourselves, to others, and to God. We become more vulnerable, and thus more authentically transparent; we begin to understand the possibility of a new sense of intimacy with our very selves as well as with God's Spirit who resides in the broken lives of others around us. Society's masks and costumes that we wear slip off more easily from bowed heads and slumped shoulders. That is why there is the sacrament of reconciliation in the early morning after being awake all night. Priests hope that confession becomes the high point of one's time at Lough Derg. It is a time of a rugged cleansing of one's entire self — body, mind, and spirit — that time in Purgatory is meant for, as we gradually — if haltingly — humbly put on Christ where once upon a time society's wardrobe fit perfectly.

It is 12:00 noon: again, time for worship. Now we reaffirm our baptismal covenant. Sagheed, a priest from Iraq, leads worship. He sprays water over all of us, and we individually make a single file for the anointment with oil on our foreheads, this time with aid of lay leaders. I am getting lost in the plethora of rituals that guides our vigil.

Ronin and I head to the Day Room, which is next to the Reading Room, again with hard wooden seats and benches. The Reading Room is so cozy, so warm, so inviting to the temptation of sleep that we both know it would be our end if we were seated in the womb-like setting.

At three in the afternoon there is another call to worship for the celebration of the Stations of the Cross. Afterward,

Ronin and I head to the dining hall. I am taught a trick to eating the toast: sprinkling sugar on it. We talk with some older women who are all veterans of Purgatory. One woman has come twenty times, while the youngest has come only twelve times. Another woman has a son living in Los Angeles, while another woman loved talking to me about New York City, a place she visited twenty years ago, but remembers as if it were just yesterday. Two younger women sit next to me, both vowing never to return to Purgatory again. As I look toward the lake a boat of pilgrims arrives for the walk.

At Night Prayers our candlelight is extinguished. All that is left is a vapor that ascends to the heavens. I hear us all breathe a collective sigh. Our vigil is over; people are taking off quickly for their respective bunks and falling asleep. A "We did it!" feeling overcomes me. At 1:00 a.m., someone cries from a bunk nearby, awaking not only the living, but the dead. I awaken again from my dreamy stupor by the bell bonging outside the men's dorm window. All the men around me slip quickly out of their beds and take the sheets off, then dash into the bathroom to shave and clean for the last few hours in Purgatory.

Even though the priest made it explicitly clear that the Stations are not to be a race, nevertheless, Ronin and I watch as a group of pilgrims sprint to St. Brigid's cross, renouncing evil, flesh, capitalism, MTV, Tony Blair, and the devil as quickly as possible. On the steps of the basilica people shove each other to get to St. Patrick's cross and quickly kiss it. Because there are so many people here, we are given the option of completing the ninth Station in the basilica, but Ronin and I choose to do it outside after the maddening crowd is finished.

The ninth time through the Stations is magical. I am invigorated by completing the daunting task before me. I no longer worry about completing the Stations, or time myself against others to see who is the quickest and the best at completing a round of prayers. Instead, I can finally enjoy the luxury of time, of not worrying about money, academic prestige, or guilt for all the sins I have committed in my life, knowingly or unknowingly. Just by being here, on this isle, in the middle of Ireland, praying, I experience a refreshing breeze of cleansing grace. I feel freedom from all things and people that may make me anxious. Patricia Hampl writes that while sin is an incident along a pilgrimage, penitence — or penance — is a trip toward life.[1]

One other man in his forties is with me in praying this last Station, and we break the unspoken rules and talk to one another while working the Stations. He comes here because he is caught up in the anxieties provoked by living the "ways of the world," as he put it, in his small Irish village. He needs to bounce out of it in order to get perspective of what is real, of what matters in his life. As we talk, we watch a father and son individually work the Stations, the son — in his forties — helping his father up and down the rough stone pathway.

An "If I can do this, I can do anything" spirit overtakes me, and I laugh out loud. In Christ, with Christ, Christ beneath me, Christ above me, Christ all over the place, spreading out, big and wide: the truthfulness of St. Patrick's prayer leaping into my consciousness like a wild stallion. Perseverance with Christly humility is the virtue that seeps through my skin and bones, inhabits my life, settles into my tissues and organs, takes up residence in my consciousness.

---

1. Patricia Hampl, "Penance," in *Signatures of Grace*, ed. T. Grady and Paula Huston (New York: Dutton, 2000), 57.

This pilgrimage has been a solitary venture, absent any sense of community, save for the commonality of the pilgrimage we had all completed individually. There is no sense of community per se, as I found in Chimayo, New Mexico, or Esquipulas, Guatemala. Here, the individual and his or her life and sins are the focus, and not the community of pilgrims. "I" am on a pilgrimage, among many other isolated individuals; "we" are not on pilgrimage together, and there is little holding us in this body, save in the common action in praying the Stations.

I skip steps and run upstairs and grab my bags. I stroll down to the foot baths, my feet slightly less tender than they were a few days earlier. The warm water cascading over my toes, sliding down the sole of the foot, my heel, over the top of my foot as I take fingers to toes and wash each inch of foot surface: it is most enjoyable, even sensual. I carefully put socks and shoes back on and walk outside. I look at the next band of pilgrims climbing the Beds, and smile, say a prayer with them as I saunter to the departing boat.

Once on the boat, I am told that if you look back, you are certain to come back to this island of Purgatory. Ronin declares that's why he's come back four times. Bravely, or foolheartedly, I look back on Purgatory, remembering I am a pilgrim for life.

Chapter Ten

THE ROAD TO DAMASCUS ... VIRGINIA

*Now as he journeyed, he approached Damascus, and sud-
denly a Light from heaven flashed about him.* — Acts 9:3

This autumn day could not have begun more beautiful:
the sun was shooting rays through the white-gray clouds,
spreading sunshine all over the orange-yellow-brown, and
black-spotted calico pattern of colored leaves carpeting the
gently undulating mountains of the Appalachian range. God
is an impressionist artist. While we — a group of amateur
hikers — were surrounded by autumn's beauty and mild
temperatures, we were also aware that the weather forecast-
ers were more foreboding: while bright sunshine bathed the
group of nine pilgrim hikers, we all knew there was the possibility of scattered afternoon thunderstorms. Like the journey
of old Saul of Tarsus, our journey began with some sense of
mystery and wonder, the cloud of unknowing surrounding
us with a hint of wonderment. And like Saul, we too were
going to go through a conversion, or what the Benedictines
call a *conversatio*, beginning a lifelong turning or ongoing
conversion as the incarnate God of creation would reveal to
one and all the pilgrimage that is the Christian life.

On this pilgrimage there were nine of us. We were an
interesting gathering of pilgrims, but then again, what gathering of pilgrims isn't interesting? There were the three older
men, of which I was one. There were the two young trail

guides, who were in their young twenties. And the other five were high-school-aged youth, who were coming along on this wilderness pilgrimage. While there was one young man who was a Boy Scout, proudly on his way to becoming an Eagle Scout, the rest of us were either novices in the way of hiking or veterans who had last picked up a forty-pound backpack some twenty years ago, or longer.

While we were expecting nearly thirty pilgrim hikers some weeks ago, this size worked out just fine for me. Since this was my first time hiking-as-pilgrimage, I was excited to see what the possibilities would be like. I was hopeful that we would find the pilgrim spirit that Annie Dillard embodied as she took a pilgrimage into the depth and heart of Tinker Creek, and the solace in the fierce landscapes that Belden Lane discovered in the dramatic landscapes of northern New Mexico. With this size group, we also had the possibility of getting to know one another in ways that a group of thirty would have made impossible, even if we had been broken up into three groups of ten. This size worked especially well as we were all novices in the act and art of being pilgrims on a wilderness trail like the Appalachian Trail.

Our route was well marked, of that we were assured. The Appalachian Trail is marked with the logo of a capital "A" over a capital "T." Besides the signs, there were white rectangular marks painted high on the trees that we would follow, leading the way forward. Finally, we followed countless footsteps of people who had been on the trail before us for many years, stamping down anything that might have wanted to grow. So we marched onward and literally upward as the trail seemed to rarely hit a plateau: we were either walking upward, even negotiating small steps on wet rocks and limbs, or zig-zagging downward for countless miles. The only time we walked on a level plain seemed to be high on a ridge back, providing us a great seat for drinking in magnificent vistas of the land around us. This would have all been a hike in the woods or a touristy escape, save for one essential ingredient that made this a pilgrimage: what made this a pilgrimage was the very purpose of our journey together, which was to learn the timeless practices, the timeworn art, and the ancient rituals of being pilgrims in this modern age.

An important point: A hike is to travel by any means possible. It could mean taking a longer walk than walking a short distance, from point A to point B. To go on a hike is to go for pleasure or exercise. But a pilgrimage is to go on a quest, a searching journey, in which pleasure or exercise are by-products of what is truly our aim: to search within ourselves and among ourselves for the God in Christ who dwells within us all. Through the physical act of searching for the often hidden God in nature's wildness, we open ourselves to the God who searches for us like the "hound of heaven," not resting until we are safely in the arms of the Savior of the world.

We left from Troutdale, Virginia, our base camp of sorts, being driven to a place that was on the "Virginia Creeper" pathway on the Appalachian Trail. We began our pilgrimage hike with a traditional "Blessing of the Pilgrim," reading the beginning of Luke 24, in which the disciples on the road to Emmaus were soon joined by a "stranger" in their quick walk away from Jerusalem, the scene of the punishment of crucifixion.

It is the same blessing that I learned when I first went to Chimayo, New Mexico, five years earlier, and its words continue to bring solace, but also open me up to the wandering of the Holy Spirit among the company of pilgrim hikers I am with this day.

As we leave this place, located in a dell, secluded away from the busy highway overhead, we pause for a moment, our forty-pound backpacks on our backs, and pose for a picture. Over each one of our heads (save for one hiker) is a blue pad for our sleeping bags: it is the only thing that is uniform about us. Front and center: the cross of Christ that we made from the twigs and branches we found in the wilderness glen. We tie it with jute, making an improvised "Eye of God" string art in the middle of the cross, where pieces of wood lie perpendicular to one another. Within the next twenty-four hours this cross will be adorned with all kinds of oak twigs, branches of pine trees, the last remains of wilderness flowers that are holding on until the first frost of the season. By the end of the pilgrimage, it is a work of godly art.

While the journey was a novel experience for me, never having combined a hike on the Appalachian Trail with the practices of pilgrimage, what made this pilgrimage most memorable was reaching our destination: Damascus, Virginia! None of us had ever been there. Of course, it wasn't the town itself that was drawing us, but the name of the town, which undoubtedly had been inspired by the Damascus mentioned in the Acts of the Apostles. Saul asked the high priest for letters to the synagogues at Damascus, as he was looking for any who belonged to "the Way," the early name for Christians (Acts 9:2). It was when Paul was coming close to Damascus that a light from heaven flashed around him, and he heard Christ asking him, "Saul, Saul, why do you persecute me?" (Acts 9:4). Finally, it was in Damascus that the man by the name of Ananias took care of Saul-turned-Paul, instructed to do so by Christ (Acts 9:10–12). More importantly, Damascus was the first place that Saul-turned-Paul began to "proclaim Jesus in the synagogues, saying 'He is the Son of God....' Saul became increasingly more powerful and confounded the Jews who lived in Damascus by proving that Jesus was the Messiah" (Acts 9:20, 22).

Our pilgrimage together was simply amazing. By this time, having been on many pilgrimages as either a participant or a guide, in a variety of lands and cultures, among pilgrims of all ages, from young children to older women and men, I find that the wonder and awe of pilgrimage is that lives are changed, no matter how brief or long the pilgrimage may be. It seems that the longer the pilgrimage is, the deeper the inner change and outward disposition, because of the time and length of experience that a person has to contemplate and live in being a witness of the Gospel. Nevertheless, within a matter of three days together, a group of individuals who came from Virginia, Tennessee, and North Carolina, who had never met before, quickly became acquaintances, gradually discovered places of commonality that showed us the way toward a kind of friendship. Through waiting for one another after steep inclines, taking slower steps over marshy lands and slippery embankments, walking quietly in slight drizzle, sharing in the beauty of vistas that caught one's breath, sitting by a fire at the end of the day, and sharing the common practices and rituals of pilgrimage, including carrying a five-foot cross of Christ which we made and adding bits and pieces of nature's beauty to the inter-woven twigs and branches, all were important in shaping us, via this pilgrimage, into a band of sisters and brothers in Christ. And when we grew tired — and we all grew tired at one point or another on the pilgrim's way — the one call that helped us along was simply this: "Remember Damascus!" The thought of reaching Damascus stayed with us through our hike-pilgrimage. In a sense, the destination this time more than others drew us to itself, as if we were metal filings and the place of Damascus was our magnet. This became even more the case the second day of the pilgrimage, which was Sunday. Whether breaking down our tents or eating our meals together, undoubtedly our conversation topic turned to Damascus. Like little children in the back of the car asking the parent "Are we there yet?" we kept looking at mile markers which would tell us, in descending order, how many miles it would take to get to Damascus: "Damascus: 8 miles.... Damascus: 5 miles." Damascus called us home.

We entered the small town of Damascus, Virginia, mid-afternoon on a Sunday. The paved path we were walking on into town was to be shared with packs of bicyclists who were passing us. We did not think we were moving slowly, but we were eclipsed one by one by a bike, with bikers of all ages, shapes, and sizes passing every one of us. The path in town was paved, running parallel with the train track. Now and then we would see a restaurant or B&B, and simply salivate, hungry as we were for a warm meal or a cold milkshake. The small mom-and-pop motels enticed us with the promise of warm showers and soft beds, something that we had missed for just these two days.

Having walked through town, thinking we were almost at the very end of town itself, I searched almost fruitlessly for a church steeple, any church steeple, for we were to end our time together at the First United Methodist Church of Damascus. Suddenly, there was a plethora of steeples: undoubtedly like many small towns the churches all gravitated toward one corner of the town, with a church on each of four corners.

But it was not to be the church steeple that drew us off the trail to let us know we had reached our destination. As God is my witness, the one who welcomed us home as we came off the Appalachian Trail, in the little town of Damascus, was Rusty! Rusty is an eighty-five-year-old former prosecuting attorney, retired from St. Petersburg, Florida, who was there to greet each one of us with the incredible welcoming address and salutation: "There is an aura of the spirit or soul of the pilgrim around this one!" embracing us gently in his arms, thus making each pilgrim feel special.

Rusty had not walked long spans of the Appalachian Trail, but he had walked El Camino, the way or path to Santiago de Compostela, from France to the seaside shrine. To commemorate the walk on the Appalachian Trail he had a walking stick with medallions on it for each state that he had walked through. At the top end of the walking stick, there was a bell slightly larger and louder than a Christmas jingle bell: his bear bell, which was meant to scare the bears. No bears would be scared by such a bell really, but it was a reminder of the wildness of this trail, even in this day and age. He gave this bell to one of the young people on the journey, who was over the moon with such a gift. It was memorable, just watching the young boy's face as the bell was being handed down, one generation to the next generation. It was a gift that embodied grace.

What was most intriguing was the house next to the church: it was a hostel for people on the Appalachian Trail, thus a ministry of the church. People were welcome from north, south, east, and west, just like God's people have been invited to sit at table in the kingdom of God in both the Old and New Testaments. As is always the truth, sharing in this Eucharist was to share in the "joyful feast of the people of God!"

Jan, the pastor of the United Methodist church in Damascus, had prepared for our coming: she had a basket of fruit, of cookies and chips; a tray of drinks. She also prepared for us the pottery cup of juice and pottery paten of bread that we would need for Holy Communion. Not only were the elements for the Lord's Supper there, but so were the people.

In our closing time, we read the conclusion of the story of the disciples on the way to Emmaus, and how their eyes were opened in the breaking of the bread, and they discerned rightly that it was the risen Christ who was once a stranger in their midst. Breaking the bread, then sharing the cup, repeating the words, "Do this in remembrance of me," all the people partook in the meal, both the pilgrims as well as those who were staying at the hostel. The community of pilgrims I had been with soon reached out to include those people who were waiting for us in Damascus. We gathered in a large circle to hear the words of the Invitation to the Lord's Table; we bowed our heads in prayer with the reading of the Great Thanksgiving, and all joined in one voice in praying the Lord's Prayer. In the breaking of the bread, we each received the bread, dipped in the cup, and celebrated our oneness with all pilgrims throughout time who have partaken in this Divine Feast, this Grand Banquet of Love.

At the end of our time together, we hugged and kissed one another good-bye. Yet this Damascus became for us like Paul's Damascus was for him: a place of change, in which the unexpected Spirit of God arose to meet us in this place, of all places. Our journey was God's gift to each one of us, showing us the beauty of nature and the beauty of friendship. Our destination was equally a gift of God's, reminding us of our ancestry with the Apostle Paul, and with all the saints who have been "on the road," where, once again, we met the risen Christ who was and is burning in our hearts and rekindling our desire.

Chapter Eleven

ACCIDENTAL PILGRIMS
ON THE ROAD TO EMMAUS

Then they told what had happened on the road, and how he had been made known to them in the breaking of the bread.
—Luke 24:35

WWJD. That's what the bracelet said: WWJD. Of course, there are plenty of jokes that soon came to embrace the simple initialed monogram: "What would Jesus Do?" soon turned into "What would Jesus Drink?" "Drive?" "Drum?" "De-Classify?" "Destroy?" or "Develop," as in a housing development. There is no end to such faddish and silly lines.

For example, for one generation of Christians there was the book — a classic on some people's bookshelves — *In His Steps.* In this book the author wrote of a small family and family business, in which everyone took on the Herculean — meaning "impossible" — task of living like Jesus Christ. Throughout the book we follow one dilemma after another that faces each person as they valiantly try but soon fail to live up to the standards of the Christ. It is an arduous task, and an arduous book, for it misses the point of Christ: it is faith, it is grace, that saves us, which is not of our own doing, but of God.

A spiritual reflection on Luke 24:13–35, preached at St. John's Presbyterian Church, Durham, North Carolina.

Each and every Christian, in each and every generation of the church, usually comes around to embrace this challenge, of imagining or trying to do what Jesus would do, as we try to live and follow his earthly steps. Why such a yearning? Freud and Jung would say it is an attempt to bond and link ourselves with a parent-figure extraordinaire, who could help us with, if not solve, all our cares and woes. And in going back to this age-old search — what would it be like to be followers in the presence of Jesus in the very days of Jesus? — we turn to the Bible, to commentaries, to preachers on television, and to theatrical movies and musicals, which lure us to imagine what clothes Jesus wore (a toga), what shoes he walked in (sandals), what his hair was like (long), his beard (close-cropped), and his build (slender).

More to the point, we are sure, vainly sure, in believing that if *we'd* been around at the time of Christ, we would have *instantly* recognized him as the Son of God, Light of Light, the Messiah, the Beloved of God. We would have been there with oil at his birth, along with the wise men; stood behind him at the Temple when he was twelve, reading the words of the Scriptures with him, but quietly; visited Joseph's carpentry house; been a fly on the wall with Martha, Mary, and Lazarus; held palm branches; been at Pilate's court shouting the correct name; and hung in there on Good Friday and Holy Saturday.

Or maybe we wouldn't.

Why?

Because Jesus was probably not that recognizable.

Wedded to the Hollywood, 1940s image of Jesus, we cannot help but imagine that that celluloid portrayal of Jesus was charismatic through and through. The lure of the beautiful Hollywood Jesus continues in each of us every day.

167

Our Jesus, the one we call Lord, was probably like every other Joseph, Peter, or Mark; his divinity was utterly unrecognizable. That is precisely why his claims to be God were considered an offense to human reason, thus demanding a leap of faith . . . and then some. Likewise, we, failing to find an idealized Christ, would have probably responded to Jesus as others did — by crucifying him. The Gospels make no bones about his ending. He died as dead as any man or woman. On the cross he had come to the last of all his moments, and because he was conscious still — alive to his death — he caught one final glimpse of the life he had all but finished living.

Who knows what he glimpsed as that life passed before him. Maybe here and there a fragment preserved for no good reason like old snapshots in a desk drawer: the play of sunlight on a wall, a half-remembered face, something somebody said. A growing sense perhaps of destiny: the holy one in the river, a gift for prayer, a gift for moving simple hearts. One hopes he remembered good times, although the Gospels record few — his visits with his friends Mary, Martha, and Lazarus and how he went to a wedding where water was turned into wine. There were the events of the last days, when a great crowd gathered to watch him enter the city on the foal, a colt, of a donkey. He knew terror in the garden. Shalom pierced through his sun-dried lips on the cross. Finished.

That is why the two disciples, two accidental pilgrims if there ever were any, failed to recognize anything about the one walking with them. They literally and figuratively didn't know who it was. They had been around for the last horrendous days of Jesus. They knew the Jesus of the crucifixion. What or who they didn't know was the Christ of all creation, who is beyond our simple, limited imagination. The dream of holiness, to help make bearable our dark nights of the soul, was in the flesh, in the spirit, in their minds, that very night.

They must have walked a good long time with their pilgrim companion. Pilgrim one and Cleopas talked to the "stranger" in their midst about what happened in Jerusalem. You can almost see the comedy in the situation as the risen Christ, the Lord of Creation, calmly asked them what actually had happened in Jerusalem. Ever the teacher, the risen Christ, was getting a firsthand account of how the world had seen and understood what had occurred. The history lesson comes in verse 27, when the stranger begins to tell them what had actually happened, beginning with Moses, all that the prophets said, and all the things about himself in the scriptures. Once a rabbi, always a rabbi.

But the power of the story is in the closing lines of this chapter in Luke. After all that had been conveyed by the two disciples, the traveling companion revealed his true nature to these befuddled, accidental pilgrims. Jesus Christ revealed himself to these two because God in Christ chose, out of love, to reveal himself, the Godhead, to them. As we read in the first letter of John, "See what love the Father has given us, that we should be called children of God; and that is what we are."

Here, for me, is where the true wonder is: in the breaking of the bread. "When he was at the table with them, he took bread, blessed and broke it, and gave it to them. Then their eyes were opened, and they recognized him; and he vanished from their sight." It is in the bread, the broken bread, a sign of a meal to be shared as we take the whole loaf and make it possible for one and all to eat from it, that we are reminded, remembered, and reconnected with the Christ.

169

And so, pilgrims of today, we will take the bread, the body of Christ, and we will break it again. The brokenness of the bread reminds us of our brokenness on the one hand. On the other hand the broken bread also reminds us of the feast of Christ's body, which nurtures and sustains us for the journey before us all. Once bread is broken it cannot be sold. It must be used, eaten, taken care of, and shared, among friends. Amen.

Epilogue

Benedictine Abbot John Main writes that a monk is a person who can carry the past with him or her, "*collect* it on his [her] *pilgrimage* [my emphasis] and transform it into the radiant present of the new creation. The monk is therefore a [person] who must make his [her] tradition more relevant to the present than mere novelty."[1]

As I write this Epilogue, I receive in the mail a card from a person in her seventies who took a class on pilgrimage with me a few months ago. She writes: "Thanks so much for leading the course on pilgrimage. I came away with lots of food for thought, and I enjoyed the others in the group. In trying to interpret the idea of the pilgrimage and carrying the cross, I've realized that life *is* a pilgrimage and we each have our cross to carry or live with."

The student who took the course on pilgrimage did what Abbot Main says a monk and all Christians do on pilgrimage: we take the memories, ideas, comments, opinions, sensations, reflections of a pilgrimage that we are on, and let these things transform our life personally, and our lives collectively, and in doing so in this "radiant present moment," make of it a new creation...or be made a new creation because of these experiences of being one of God's pilgrim people.

---

1. John Main, "The Witness of Monastic Prayer," *Monastic Studies* 18 (Christmas, 1988): 31.

The student took the experience of being on pilgrimage, and that experience of carrying the cross we made in the class gave her a way of interpreting her life in the body of Christ anew: life *is* a pilgrimage, and we each have our cross to carry or live with.

In closing, I can say that, having been on pilgrimage numerous times, with more opportunities making themselves known all the time, there is no doubt that the tradition, the practices of pilgrimage, do not belong in the category of "mere novelty." Instead, it has been the intentional pilgrimages that I have been on that have given me an invaluable framework and profoundly practical script by which I can better understand and appreciate what I encounter in my personal life, the life of congregations in which I am the pastor or the congregant, and the life of the classrooms and lecture halls in which I teach.

To put it more simply: going on pilgrimage has become a portal, a window, by which I now understand better than ever before that the Christian life we all live is one of a pilgrimage. In this real-life, lifelong pilgrimage, every one of us is called to be fully and authentically ourselves. In such authenticity we encounter more fully the Holy Spirit who dwells within and among us.

The lessons learned from being on actual pilgrimages will be with me for years to come. First, I have come to learn that people of all ages can learn something from being on pilgrimage. I have been on pilgrimage with toddlers and young children, and have enjoyed taking young people between the ages of ten and fourteen on pilgrimage. When I went on pilgrimage with middle-school aged children at Massanetta Springs Middle School conference in Virginia, the way that the young people understood pilgrimage was as a "religious hike" one child told me, in which they related well to the "pilgrimage" that the Hobbits and humans took in Tolkein's Lord of the Rings cycle. The twelve groups of young pilgrims I walked with made beautiful crosses that were simply works of natural art. Likewise, I have been on pilgrimage with people in their high school years at Duke Youth Academy in Durham, North Carolina, with classes from Duke Divinity School and Duke Lay Academy, as well as with people in the senior years of life, and they all have come to experience something new and different in being on pilgrimage.

I have come to appreciate the way that Christian community is formed around the presence of people with disabilities on pilgrimage. I have been on pilgrimage with people in wheelchairs in natural settings, with people working together to lift wheel chairs, and people, over rocks and creeks, experiencing together a critique of the less-than-accessible paths while learning to act as a community of stewards.

Second, I am always amazed when the impulse to be on pilgrimage or the symbols of previous pilgrimages make themselves known in my daily life. For example, I was on a mission trip with Presbyterian college students from North Carolina, traipsing around Puerto Plata's Catholic church, when I looked up at the Christ figure in the front of the church and beheld El Cristo Negro — in the Dominican Republic! I smiled at seeing this Black Christ, remembering well the Black Christ in Guatemala, and the people I have met since being there. In Walsingham, England, recently, with former students from pilgrimage classes at Duke Divinity School, we were all abuzz about the various parts of the shrine to Our Lady of Walsingham in that small English town. Wherever I roam, I am bound to meet a symbol, a sign, an image, or a song that reminds me that life is a pilgrimage. More recently my trips to Thailand, Cambodia, and Japan helped me think more about the universality of pilgrimage among the religions of the world.

And lastly, I rely more and more upon understanding that life *is* a pilgrimage, taught to me by Christ in others, the communion of saints, friends, strangers, enemies, and spontaneous acquaintances, along with all of creation. While I may have begun this all as an "accidental pilgrim," I now know that there was no accident involved. Our calling as Christians is to be what we are called to be in the Acts of the Apostles: people of the Way (9:2). The places that I have gone on pilgrimages and the people I have met have all provided for me many lessons about being on a lifelong pilgrimage wherever I am in this world. What I attempted to do in this book of essays is simply share my experience with pilgrims in different parts of the world. I do so in the hope of making connection with other pilgrims in the world, who know that we worship as God's pilgrim church, following forevermore the Pilgrim Christ.